आ नो भद्रा.
Let noble thoughts

-i

BHAVAN'S BOOK UNIVERSITY

115

BHAGAVAD GITA

by
C. RAJAGOPALACHARI

BOOKS BY

C. RAJAGOPALACHARI

PUBLISHED BY THE BHAVAN

Ramayana

Mahabharata

Rajaji's Speeches Vol. I

Rajaji's Speeches Vol. II

Hinduism: Doctrine and Way of Life

Bhagavad Gita

Stories for the Innocent

Kural — The Great Book of Tiru-Valluvar

Upanishads

Our Culture

Bhaja Govindam

Gandhiji's Teachings & Philosophy

Avvaiar (The Great Tamil Poet)

Kathopanishad (Tamil)

Rescue Democracy from Money Power

Bhagavad Gita (Hindi)

Upanishads (Hindi-cum-English Edition)

Bhajagovind (Kannada)

BHAVAN'S BOOK UNIVERSITY

BHAGAVAD GITA

C. RAJAGOPALACHARI

2014

BHARATIYA VIDYA BHAVAN

Kulapati Munshi Marg

Mumbai - 400 007

1st Edition : 1963	*13th Edition : 1997*
2nd Edition : 1964	*14th Edition : 1999*
3rd Edition : 1967	*15th Edition : 2001*
4th Edition : 1974	*16th Edition : 2003*
5th Edition : 1975	*17th Edition : 2005*
6th Edition : 1978	*18th Edition : 2006*
7th Edition : 1982	*19th Edition : 2008*
8th Edition : 1989	*20th Edition : 2010*
9th Edition : 1991	*21st Edition : 2011*
10th Edition : 1993	*22nd Edition : 2012*
11th Edition : 1995	*23rd Edition : 2013*
12th Edition : 1996	*24th Edition : 2014*

Price Rs. 70.00

PRINTED IN INDIA

By Atul Goradia at Siddhi Printers, 13/14, Bhabha Building,
13th Khetwadi Lane, Mumbai - 400 004, and Published by
P. V. Sankarankutty, Joint Director, for the Bharatiya
Vidya Bhavan, Kulapati Munshi Marg, Mumbai - 400 007.
E-Mail : bhavan@bhavans.info ● Web-site : www.bhavans.info

KULAPATI'S PREFACE

THE Bharatiya Vidya Bhavan—that Institute of Indian Culture in Bombay—needed a Book University, a series of books which, if read, would serve the purpose of providing higher education. Particular emphasis, however, was to be put on such literature as revealed the deeper impulsions of India. As a first step, it was decided to bring out in English 100 books, 50 of which were to be taken in hand almost at once. Each book was to contain from 200 to 250 pages.

- It is our intention to publish the books we select, not only in English, but also in the following Indian languages: Hindi, Bengali, Gujarati, Marathi, Tamil, Telugu, Kannada and Malayalam.

The scheme, involving the publication of 900 volumes, requires ample funds and an all-India organisation. The Bhavan is exerting its utmost to supply them.

The objectives for which the Bhavan stands are the reintegration of the Indian culture in the light of modern knowledge and to suit our present-day needs and the resuscitation of its fundamental values in their pristine vigour.

Let me make our goal more explicit:

We seek the dignity of man, which necessarily implies the creation of social conditions which would allow him freedom to evolve along the lines of his own temperament

and capacities; we seek the harmony of
individual efforts and social relations, not in
any makeshift way, but within the frame-work
of the Moral Order; we seek the creative art of
life, by the alchemy of which human limitations
are progressively transmuted, so that man may
become the instrument of God, and is able to
see Him in all and all in Him.

The world, we feel, is too much with us.
Nothing would uplift or inspire us so much as
the beauty and aspiration such books can
teach.

In this series, therefore, the literature of
India, ancient and modern, will be published in
a form easily accessible to all. Books in other
literatures of the world, if they illustrate the
principles we stand for, will also be included.

This common pool of literature, it is
hoped, will enable the reader, eastern or
western, to understand and appreciate
currents of world thought, as also the
movements of the mind in India, which though
they flow through different linguistic channels,
have a common urge and aspiration.

Fittingly, the Book University's first
venture is the *Mahabharata,* summarised by
one of the greatest living Indians, C.
Rajagopalachari; the second work is on a
section of it, the *Gita,* by H.V. Divatia, an
eminent jurist and a student of philosophy.
Centuries ago, it was proclaimed of the
Mahabharata. "What is not in it, is nowhere."
After twenty-five centuries, we can use the
same words about it. He who knows it not,

knows not the heights and depths of the soul; he misses the trials and tragedy and the beauty and grandeur of life.

The *Mahabharata* is not a mere epic; it is a romance, telling the tale of heroic men and women and of some who were divine; it is a whole literature in itself, containing a code of life, a philosophy of social and ethical relations, and speculative thought on human problems that is hard to rival; but, above all, it has for its core the *Gita*, which is, as the world is beginning to find out, the noblest of scriptures and the grandest of sagas in which the climax is reached in the wondrous Apocalypse in the Eleventh Canto.

Through such books alone the harmonies underlying true culture, I am convinced, will one day reconcile the disorders of modern life.

I thank all those who have helped to make this new branch of the Bhavan's activity successful.

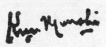

PREFACE

IT is a matter for great regret that the young men and women of our Universities know very much less about the *Gita* and the principles of Hindu religion than the undergraduates of European Universities know about the Bible and the principles of the Christian faith. We inherit in Hindu religion a body of thought which, in the opinion of those best fitted to judge, is the product of the highest efforts of intellect and imagination that ever were turned in that direction. Young men and women of any Western nation, had they inherited our philosophy, would have been as proud of it as of an empire.

This book has been written mainly to serve as a handbook for students. Reading these pages, if they find any thought in the text or in the explanation not satisfying, or wanting in clarity, or such as evokes disagreement, they should pursue the matter discussing it with fellow-students or consulting scholars. No Indian can consider himself as having attained a liberal education if he has not a sound knowledge of the principles of the great religious philosophy for which India is famous throughout the civilized world.

This little book is an attempt like what the father in the old story did with his sons, who were told to dig for treasure in the family garden. The gold was indeed found; not as coined treasure hidden away in a pot but as the reward of toil, a plentiful crop which the garden yielded for the digging. There is nothing in what the writer has himself written, but if the readers are induced to dig, the *Gita*, our precious patrimony, will yield a rich harvest for the striving soul.

Many suggestions were made after the issue of the first edition, to make subsequent issues more useful, for example that parallel quotations and *Upanishad* sources may be given, and that a bibliography may be added. All these may be very useful, but I have not accepted these suggestions, as I intend that this book should continue to be a beginner's handbook, and I do not wish to aim at making it anything like a book for scholars.

C. R.

INTRODUCTORY

THE *Gita* is one of the most authoritative sources of Hindu doctrine and ethics, and is accepted as such by Hindus of all denominations. A study of even selections from it, strengthened by earnest meditation, will enable young men and women to understand the religion of our fathers, which is the background of all the noble philosophy, art, literature and civilization that we have inherited.

There are many excellent translations of the *Gita* in English and in the Indian spoken languages. For scholars, the commentaries of Sri Sankaracharya and other great religious teachers are mines of knowledge before which any modern notes are but chaff. The following pages are intended for students who have not the equipment and time for studying the original text with any of these great commentaries.

The Gita is a chapter in the *Mahabharata*. It begins by describing the agitation of Arjuna when he saw men arrayed on either side for mutual slaughter, and into this scene is fitted the exposition of Hindu *Dharma*, in terms of what Krishna spoke to Arjuna in order to quell his agitation and clear his doubts. Krishna speaks throughout the *Gita* as God himself.

In spite of what is stated in the previous paragraph, and the beauty and appropriateness of the background conceived by the bold unrivalled imagination of the ancient author, the student should note that the *Gita* as a scripture of Hinduism stands apart from the *Mahabharata*. The context has rightly receded into insignificance and has practically disappeared in orthodox Hindu interpretation. To take the battle of Kurukshetra literally and to interpret all that is said in the *Gita* in the light of the motive of the particular scene would not only not help the student to understand the *Gita* aright, but may even lead him to error. It is true that the teachings in the *Gita* being of universal validity would also be applicable to the *Mahabharata* scene and must help to solve Arjuna's problems and doubts. But we shall fail to understand the teaching aright if we are obsessed by the particular scene and seek to interpret the general by the particular. It is a common practice in Sanskrit literature to provide great works with such or other prologues. It would be a cumbersome process to convert the whole of the *Mahabharata* story into a sustained allegory in order to save the *Bhagavad-Gita* from being an incitement to violence. We should forget the battle-scene when we study the *Gita* as a scripture of *Sanatana Dharma*.

There are eighteen *adhyayas* in the *Gita* and seven hundred *slokas* in all. In the following pages 226 *slokas* are quoted. A study of them is enough to give a fairly good grasp of the *Bhagavad-Gita*.

The *Bhagavad-Gita* professes to give nothing new beyond what has previously been taught by the *Upanishads*. It contents itself with a synthesis of the older teachings. This book does not propose to give any new interpretation of the *Bhagavad-Gita*. Let the reader not expect to find in the following pages any old interpretations controverted, any newly invented explanations. This little book aims at a simplified presentation of the Gita content, and at bringing it within a small compass so as to enable the modern student to understand, in the midst of his other studies, the faith, discipline and ideals that lighted the path of life for our forefathers, and to which is given the name *Sanatana Dharma* or Hinduism.

A little knowledge of the laws of nature and the wonders of science, specially when that knowledge is acquired second-hand, without the chastening influence of effort and investigation, acts as a wine on some natures. Their sense of proportion is unset. The unknown is not only unknown but ceases to exist for them. Holy books and scriptures seem to them ancient folly; nay worse, they are looked upon as instruments and deliberate devices for the practice of fraud. But those who have struggled to obtain a deeper knowledge of the physical sciences and who, therefore, know enough to retain their sense of proportion and judgment know that the vast unknown is ever so much more than what is known and that while human intelligence may bring under its domain more and more as time goes on, there is a residue that cannot be either ignored or brought under the sway of man's intelligence. Men of science not only preserve their humility but on account of their very knowledge of some of the secrets of nature, contemplate with increased humility and reverence that which must ever remain outside the pale of human analysis.

The cause of all causes, the law of all laws cannot be seized by the highest effort of human reasoning or investigation. Human reason is so perfectly fashioned and rounded off that there is no room for any sense of limitation. But the fact remains that the part cannot comprehend the whole, however excellent it may be shaped. The symbol of the serpent with the tail in its mouth as if swallowing itself illustrates the limitation of the human mind in its efforts to grasp the All. Even a giant cannot stand on a platform and lift it also. We cannot jump off the ultimate cause on which we stand and on which we depend for every motion of the mind, in order that we may get round it or measure it.

This limitation of human knowledge is a familiar boundary in scientific and philosophical investigations. Dive into any truth or investigate any phenomenon or examine any distinction deep enough, and at a certain point we reach the unknowable and further progress is stopped. We strike against God, so to say, in everything. The Unknowable is all-pervading. The known and knowable make up but a thin surface-crust over a mystery-sphere of infinite dimensions. Religions and holy books, and the sayings and doings of holy men deal with this infinite unknown, not as science deals with matter, but in a different way which is also the only possible way.

It may be asked why anyone should worry about the unknown. Of what use is it? The answer is that to ignore the real is foolish. The unknown is no less real because it is unknown. We know this much about it, that it is there and has profound relation to all that exists including ourselves, How then can we ignore it? The gap in human perception, we know, is not a void but filled with the most important reality, although we cannot dive into it, analyse it or understand it. In the material world, does not the mathematician deal with quantities that are too great or too small for definition, and with expressions that are for the human understanding wholly unreal?

Infinity, zero and surds are not neglected in mathematics, but go greatly to make up a science which actually helps engineers and mechanics to build real and useful construction. The insoluble and the infinite are thus neither unreal nor useless even for practical life. What is said in the *Gita*, the *Upanishads* and other holy books of the world may often be not as precise or clear as we would want it to be. The explanations are not as satisfying as the proofs we find in the physical sciences. This is necessarily so because the matter is wholly different and the approach and methods of application also must differ. Things within the domain of human reasoning can be defined and proved. But for

the understanding of things beyond, faith and
meditation have to function. The scriptures and
holy books may be looked upon as helps to
assist reverent meditation, by which alone the
human mind can get glimpses into the truth
beyond. By cultivation of purity of mind and
action, and by meditation and prayer, what
sounded first but as an empty jingle of
antithetic phrases gets substance and
meaning. What was obscure gets a strange and
new light by which we may see though dimly,
and though, even that, we may not all be able
to relate to others. Thus it was our fathers saw,
and thus again we may also see.

A reverent spirit is necessary to
understand any religion. To start with a
suspicion that the founders and teachers of
Religion in any land were skilful deceivers,
interested in some scheme of self-advancement
or the advantage of some particular class, and
that the rest of the people were duped to regard
these deceivers with unbounded reverence and
affection, is foolish in the extreme. The mass of
the people of ancient days, from whom, indeed,
we have inherited all the intellect we possess
were as practical as we are, were as interested
in knowing the truth about men and things as
we are, and were, if it may be so put, as
suspicious as we are. They had probably as
much intellectual acumen as we have, and had
indeed more time to examine men and things.
To believe that they were duped and that
among them there were not men intelligent and
bold enough to prevent the mischief is to
proceed on a wholly wrong assumption. The

religions that have commanded the devotion of successive generations of normal human beings in any country have done so because by direct personal contact at first, and by experience handed down as tradition from one generation to another, the founders and teachers of the religions were known to their contemporaries to be good, sincere and deep-thinking men, worthy of being followed. It is not merely wrong to display the detective-police mentality when studying a religion; it incapacitates one even to understand it. Undoubtedly personal and class interests have perverted religion as they have perverted other institutions. But to confuse the later with the earlier and to impute fraud to the source is an unscientific attitude of mind in the investigation of truth. The *Rishis* of our land, who have bequeathed to us great thoughts, were *Rishis* and no less. It is in a spirit of reverent affection that we should approach the study of an ancient scripture.

CONTENTS

CHAPTER I

THE SOUL

[Adhyaya II—Slokas 11-12-13, 17, 20, 22, 24, 25,
and 30. Adhyaya XIII—Slokas 26, 32 and 33.]

THE first step in religion is the realization of
the existence of an entity behind the apparent
body, *i.e.,* the Soul. The visible body is not the
whole reality. There is in it an unseen but ever-
active master of the house, the *Dehi* (देही), the
possessor of the body, whose existence we
should realize before we can live the true life.
This entity, the Self, should not be confused
with the intangible functions of the brain. It is
not mere Thought, Perception, Emotion, Will or
Discriminative Intelligence. These are all but
functions of the physical body. The Soul is an
entity apart from and behind all these
functions. It is not seated in any particular
part of the body but pervades the whole of it
and all the senses, unaffected by the law of
"extension" even as ether was taken by the
physicists to pervade the whole of space and
matter. Not only man, but every animal and
plant, every living thing, has a Soul. The body
is but the field of action, the *Kshetra*, in which
resides the Soul, who is the *Kshetri*, or
Kshetrajna.

The Soul does not cease to exist when the body dies and is buried, burnt or eaten up by wild birds or beasts. Grief over death is foolish, the Soul being incapable of death. It is the body that is cast off in death even as we cast off old clothes.

श्री भगवानुवाच

अशोच्यानन्वशोचस्त्वं प्रज्ञावादांश्च भाषसे ।
गतासूनगतासूंश्च नानुशोचन्ति पण्डिता: ॥

THE LORD SAID

You grieve for those who are not to be grieved for, yet you speak words of seeming wisdom. The enlightened grieve neither for the living nor for the dead.

II-11

न त्वेवाहं जातु नासं न त्वं नेमे जनाधिपा: ।
न चैव न भविष्याम: सर्वे वयमत: परम् ॥

At no time was I non-existent, nor thou, nor these chiefs of men, nor shall any of us ever cease to be hereafter.

II-12

देहिनोऽस्मिन्यथा देहे कौमारं यौवनं जरा ।
तथा देहान्तरप्राप्तिर्धीरस्तत्र न मुह्यति ॥

As the Soul dwelling in the body goes through childhood, youth and old age, so it moves on another body; the wise are not disturbed in mind over it.

II-13

अविनाशि तु तद्विद्धि येन सर्वमिदं ततम् ।
विनाशमव्ययस्यास्य न कश्चित्कर्तुमर्हति ॥

Know that to be indestructible by
which all these living beings here on
earth are pervaded. No one can work
the destruction of that imperishable
entity.

II-17

न जायते म्रियते वा कदाचि-
न्नायं भूत्वा भविता वा न भूयः ।
अजो नित्यः शाश्वतोऽयं पुराणो
न हन्यते हन्यमाने शरीरे ॥

The Soul is not born, nor does it
die; nor having been, ceases at any time
to be; unborn, unchanging, ever-
abiding, primeval, it is not killed when
the body is killed.

II-20

वासांसि जीर्णानि यथा विहाय
नवानि गृह्णाति नरोऽपराणि ।
तथा शरीराणि विहाय जीर्णा-
न्यन्यानि संयाति नवानि देही ।

Men cast off worn-out garments
and put on new ones. Even so the Soul
casts off worn-out bodies, and enters
into new bodies.

II-22

अच्छेद्योऽयमदाह्योऽयमक्लेद्योऽशोष्य एव च ।
नित्यः सर्वगतः स्थाणुरचलोऽयं सनातनः ॥

It is uncleavable, it is incombustible, it cannot be drenched or dried up; it abides for ever, all-pervasive, stable, immovable, primeval.

II-24

अव्यक्तोऽयमचिन्त्योऽयमविकार्योऽयमुच्यते ।
तस्मादेवं विदित्वैनं नानुशोचितुमर्हसि ॥

It is declared about it that it is unmanifest, incomprehensible and immutable. Knowing it as such you should not grieve.

II-25

देही नित्यमंबध्योऽयं देहे सर्वस्य भारत ।
तस्मात्सर्वाणि भूतानि न त्वं शोचितुमर्हसि ॥

The Soul that thus dwells in the body of everyone is ever-abiding and invulnerable. It is not for you, therefore, to grieve for any creature.

II-30

It is not as if men have souls and not beasts. All living beings and plants also have souls.

यावत्सञ्जायते किञ्चित्सत्त्वं स्थावरजंगमम् ।
क्षेत्रक्षेत्रज्ञसंयोगात्तद्विद्धि भरतर्षभ ॥

Whatsoever life is born, fixed or moving, know that it comes to be from the union of body and Soul.

XIII-26

Where is the Soul lodged? Is it in the head, or in the region of the heart, or somewhere else? It is all-pervading and is not to be located in any particular part or organ of the body.

यथा सर्वगतं सौक्ष्म्यत्तदाकाशं नोपलिप्यते ।
सर्वत्रावस्थितो देहे तथाऽऽत्मा नोपलिप्यते ॥

As the all-pervading ether is too subtle to be affected by anything it pervades, so abiding everywhere in the body the Self remains unaffected.

XIII-32

यथा प्रकाशयत्येक: कृत्स्नं लोकमिमं रवि: ।
क्षेत्रं क्षेत्री तथा कृत्स्नं प्रकाशयति भारत ॥

As the one sun irradiates the whole earth, so the Soul irradiates the whole body.

XIII-33

Chapter II

KARMA

[Adhyaya XV—Slokas 7-9. Adhyaya XIII—
Slokas 19-21.]

THE relationship of the individual Soul to the
Supreme Spirit on the one hand and to the
material body on the other is to be gathered
from the verses taken up for study now. The
Supreme Spirit may be said to dwell within the
individual Soul and to irradiate it as even the
latter dwells within and illumines the material
body. We read in the previous chapter that the
Soul successively takes various visible forms
and "becomes" man, bird, beast or plant. The
Supreme Spirit may be said similarly to
"become" or "transform" itself into numerous
souls at the same time. The individual Soul
may also be looked upon as a fragment of the
Universal Spirit, but the transcendental nature
of the original is such that fragmentation does
not affect its integrity. Further attempts at
exact definition of the relationship of the
individual Soul to the Supreme Spirit will take
us into the learned controversies of Dwaita,
Adwaita and Visishtadwaita philosophies.
Bhagavad-Gita does not discuss this question
but, like the *Upanishads*, lends itself as
authority to all these schools of thought. The

doctrine of *Karma*, the law that governs the individual Soul, is accepted by all the three schools.

The Soul's dwelling place is a casing of body which includes the senses and the mind. This casing is made out of and has its basis in the world of matter. At death, that is, when the Soul departs from one such body, it takes with it a load of character or *Gunas* as developed by the activities so far gone through. This makes the start for the next body. The Soul carries the *Gunas* in subtle form in its passage from one life to another, as the wind takes with it the fragrance from the bowers through which it passes.

ममैवांशो जीवलोके जीवभूत: सनातन: ।
मन:षष्ठानीन्द्रियाणि प्रकृतिस्थानि कर्षति ॥

A fragment of Mine own Self becomes in the world of living things an immortal Soul. It attracts to itself the five senses and a controlling mind, all six established in matter.

XV-7

शरीरं यदवाप्नोति यच्चाप्युत्क्रामतीश्वर: ।
गृहीत्वैतानि संयाति वायुर्गन्धानिवाशयात् ॥

The Soul, when it takes up lordship over a body and when it leaves it, takes these with it as the wind takes fragrances from bower to bower.

XV-8

श्रोत्रं चक्षु: स्पर्शनं च रसनं घ्राणमेव च ।
अधिष्ठाय मनश्चायं विषयानुपसेवते ॥

Using the ear, the eye, and the organs of touch, taste and smell, and the mind also, it enjoys the objects of the senses.

XV-9

It is this contact with the objects of the senses, and the attractions and attachments thereto that in subtle form hang on to the Soul and become its *Karmic* load. No explanation or theory in regard to the ultimate cause of things can be free from objections or difficulties from the rationalist point of view. But, on the assumption of an immortal Soul as the basis of personality no theory can be formulated more in conformity with the known laws of nature than the Hindu doctrine of *Karma*, Man evolves himself exactly according to his actions, the process being unbroken by death and passing on to the next life. This, the most important doctrine in Hindu religion, is the application in the moral sphere of the law of conservation of energy, and indeed both may be looked upon as parts of one law. *Karma* is the rule of the law, so to say, in the spiritual world. Cause and effect must be equivalent. As death is only disintegration of the body, and not of the Soul, the law of cause and effect, so far as the Soul is concerned, continues to operate beyond death. The death of the body does not operate as a bankruptcy court. The old account is carried over.

The tiniest pebble thrown into water produces a ripple. The disturbance is carried onward in ever-widening circles on the water.

One ripple may cut across, add itself to, and be merged in another, increasing or reducing it, but not the tiniest movement can go for naught. Likewise also do all our acts—and acts include thoughts— produce results. The most transient and secret thought entertained in the mind ruffles the calm of the Spirit Universal, and the disturbance has to be worked off.

Over and above the effect on others and apart from any question of reward or punishment, we can see, without the help of any doctrine, that every thought or act, good or bad, has at once an effect on oneself. Every motion of the mind deals a stroke with chisel and mallet, whether one wants it or not, on one's own character and its evolution is made better or worse thereby. If I think evil today, I think it more readily and persistently tomorrow and likewise is it with good thoughts. If I control or calm myself, it becomes more spontaneous, more easy next time; and this goes on progressively. At death, the Hindu doctrine says, whatever character has been hammered out by the thoughts and deeds and repentances of the life that is closed continues to attach itself as the initial start of character for the Soul in its next journey.

Karma is not Fatalism. It is not an arbitrary and external agency which makes personal effort of no avail. On the contrary, the theory places one's evolution is one's own hands completely, and even death does not interfere with the progress of effort. We shall revert to this aspect of Karma in Chapters VII and VIII.

It is well known that physical characteristics and mental traits are passed on from parents to children. This heredity does not explain what is sought to be explained by the law of *Karma*. Bodies are shaped by heredity, but not Souls. The Soul has no father or mother, but is self-existent. Any Soul may be lodged in any body in which it has earned the fitness to function. Bodies are only the tenements provided for souls even as engineers may build in similar or varying types for citizens to choose and live in, according to their needs. A house may be improved or even damaged by the occupant. The next person who comes into the tenements does so because it suits his own condition. A father may ruin the coming son's body, but which soul is to come as that son depends on the stage reached in the *Karmic* evolution of that Soul. When a son is born to parents he appears to inherit their physical and mental characteristics, but in reality what he inherits is his own previous life's accumulation, by reason of which he is embodied as son to such parents. The *aurasa* son is such only in the physical body. In the Soul, even an *aurasa* son is, so to say, but an adopted son. The law of heredity does not dispense with or interfere with the operation of the law of *Karma*.

Besides XV-7, 8 and 9 already quoted the following *Slokas* may be studied in this connection:—

प्रकृतिं पुरुषं चैव विद्ध्यनादी उभावपि ।
विकारांश्च गुणांश्चैव विद्धि प्रकृतिसम्भवान् ॥

Know that matter and Soul are both without beginning; and that all material forms, phenomena and qualities come out of matter,

XIII-19

कार्यकारणकर्तृत्वे हेतुः प्रकृतिरुच्यते ।
पुरुषः सुखदुःखानां भोक्तृत्वे हेतुरुच्यते ॥

Out of material nature are produced the means and effects; but the Soul has brought them about and reaps the pleasure and pain.

XIII-20

पुरुषः प्रकृतिस्थो हि भुङ्क्ते प्रकृतिजान्गुणान् ।
कारणं गुणसङ्गोऽस्य सदसद्योनिजन्मसु ॥

The Soul established in matter enjoys the qualities born of matter; attachment of this enjoyment is the cause of its births in good and evil wombs.

XIII-21

....
....
....

CHAPTER III

GOD AND NATURE

[Adhyaya VII—Slokas 4-14, 25 and 27.
Adhyaya IX—Slokas 4, 6, 8, 10 and 16-19.
Adhyaya XV—Slokas 16-18.]

WE shall continue in the next chapter our study of the *Gita*-teaching as to how to live. It will be helpful to pause here to contemplate on the Hindu interpretation of the riddle of the Universe, the great "open secret" which has baffled man ever since he began to think deeply, and which must ever remain an insoluble paradox. This involves a study of the 7th, 9th and 15th *Adhyayas* of the *Gita.*

All the physical elements of nature, including the material bodies of animate beings and their sensory and mental functions, may be grouped together forming the ever-changing physical aspect of the universe. This is called *Prakriti* (प्रकृति). Behind the animate is the soul that dwells within each being and animates it. Behind all again is the Supreme Being whose power it is that holds together all the changes visible in one organic existence. He dwells within and supports and moves everything, but exists apart from all.

The universe moves according to what are known as the laws of nature. This code of nature is but the manifestation of the Supreme Will. God Himself is not seen as such and as a whole. What we see of Him we are content to call by the name of physical and moral laws, and life proceeds as if wholly independent of God.

भूमिरापोऽनलो वायु: खं मनो बुद्धिरेव च ।
अहंकार इतीयं मे भिन्ना प्रकृतिरष्टधा ॥

Earth, water, fire, air, ether, thought, reasoning and consciousness of individuality — these are eightfold divisions of My nature.

VII-4

अपरेयमितस्त्वन्यां प्रकृतिं विद्धि मे पराम् ।
जीवभूतां महाबाहो ययेदं धार्यते जगत् ॥

This physical nature that I have described is My inferior manifestation. My other and higher nature is the life-principle by which the universe is upheld.

VII-5

एतद्योनीनि भूतानि सर्वाणीत्युपधारय ।
अहं कृत्स्नस्य जगत: प्रभव: प्रलयस्तथा ॥

Understand that these two constitute the womb of all beings. I am the origin of the whole universe and that into which it dissolves.

VII-6

मत्त: परतरं नान्यत्किंञ्चिदस्ति धनञ्जय ।
मयि सर्वमिदं प्रोतं सूत्रे मणिगणा इव ॥

There is naught whatsoever
beyond Me. All this universe hangs
together on Me, as pearls on a string.

VII-7

The dependence of all things and beings
in Nature on the Supreme Spirit is illustrated
in the following four slokas:

रसोऽहमप्सु कौन्तेय प्रभाऽस्मि शशिसूर्ययो: ।
प्रणव: सर्ववेदेषु शब्द: खे पौरुषं नृषु ॥

I am the taste in water, I am the
radiance in the sun and the moon, I
am the sacred OM in all the Vedas; I
am sound in space; I am virility in men.

VII-8

पुण्यो गन्ध: पृथिव्यां च तेजश्चास्मि विभावसौ ।
जीवनं सर्वभूतेषु तपश्चास्मि तपस्विषु ॥

I am the sweet fragrance of the
earth and the heat in the fire; the life
in all beings, the austerity in ascetics.

VII-9

बीजं मां सर्वभूतानां विद्धि पार्थ सनातनम् ।
बुद्धिर्बुद्धिमतामस्मि तेजस्तेजस्विनामहम् ॥

Know Me as the seed primeval of
all beings. I am the *buddhi* of the wise,
the splendour of the illustrious.

VII-10

बलं बलवतामस्मि कामरागविवर्जितम् ।
धर्माविरुद्धो भूतेषु कामोऽस्मि भरतर्षभ ॥

I am the strength of the strong,
when it is untainted by desire and
passion. I am Love that moves all
beings, when it is not against *Dharma*.

VII-11

ये चैव सात्त्विका भावा राजसास्तामसाश्च ये ।
मत्त एवेति तान्विद्धि न त्वहं तेषु ते मयि ॥

Know that purity, passion and
inertia are all from Me. I am not affected
by these conditions, but they rest in
Me.

VII-12

त्रिभिर्गुणमयैर्भावैरेभि: सर्वमिदं जगत् ।
मोहितं नाभिजानाति मामेभ्य: परमव्ययम् ॥

All this world, deluded as it is by
the play of these three conditions,
ignores Me, who transcend these and
am ever-abiding.

VII-13

दैवी ह्येषा गुणमयी मम माया दुरत्यया ।
मामेव ये प्रपद्यन्ते मायामेतां तरन्ति ते ॥

This divine *maya*, operated by Me
and founded on the play of qualities,
is hard to overcome; but they who seek
refuge in Me cross over this illusion.

VII-14

नाहं प्रकाश: सर्वस्य योगमायासमावृत: ।
मूढोऽयं नाभिजानाति लोको मामजमव्ययम् ॥

I am concealed from view by this
illusion of creative activity. This
ignorant world does not know Me, who
have neither birth nor ending.

VII-25

इच्छाद्वेषसमुत्थेन द्वन्द्वमोहेन भारत ।
सर्वभूतानि संमोहं सर्गे यान्ति परन्तप ॥

Deceived by the opposing forces
of attraction and repulsion, all creation
lives and moves in delusion.

VII-27

द्राविमौ पुरुषौ लोके क्षरश्चाक्षर एव च ।
क्षर: सर्वाणि भूतानि कूटस्थोऽक्षर उच्यते ॥

There are two elements in all
beings, the one changing and the other
unchangeable. All animate form is
Kshara, the *Akshara* is the presiding
spirit.

XV-16

उत्तम: पुरुषस्त्वन्य: परमात्मेत्युदाहृत: ।
यो लोकत्रयमाविश्य बिभर्त्यव्यय ईश्वर: ॥

The highest principle is, indeed,
to be distinguished, described as the
Supreme Self, He who pervades and
sustains the three worlds, the Eternal
Lord.

XV-17

यस्मात्क्षरमतीतोऽहमक्षरादपि चोत्तम: ।
अतोऽस्मि लोके वेदे च प्रथित: पुरुषोत्तम: ॥

Since I transcend the changeable
as well as the unchangeable, I am
known in common parlance as well as
proclaimed in the Vedas as the
Supreme Spirit.

XV-18

Notwithstanding the fact that God
supports and governs all, we are ignorant of it,
as the process of His governance is inclusive of
ourselves and all our perceptions, thoughts,
reasonings and emotions. The laws of nature
are the will of God. His will is manifested in the
shape of what we see directly or by
investigation but which we choose to call by
the name of Truth or Law of Nature. God is the
Law, and the Law is He. He rules through the
Law, and it seems as if the Law rules and not
He. The two are not different, nor can there
ever be a variation between them.

The following analogy may serve to
explain this identification of the will of God
with the laws of nature.

Suppose a magician creates a tank of
water and by the same magic fills it with fish
and other aquatic animals with some
understanding though limited. The fish must
take the water and the tank and all the
conditions of their life in the magic tank as
"natural", and do not know that it is all but the
magician's will, quite as much as they
themselves are the will of the magician. Even if

he had created, not water and fish, but kerosene and fish living therein, and even if the kerosene changed into water and the water into kerosene on alternate days, the knowing fish would have taken it all as "natural" and made a synthesis of all that they observed, and mentally codified it into a body of natural laws. They would be incognizant of the real author and controller. In the same way do the laws of physical nature hide God, though they are but the manifestation of His will. So perfect is His rule that He disappears from the scene, but He is ever present in the Law itself.

The will of God acts as the continuous natural creative force of the world, *Yoga-Maya,* as it is termed in VII-25, and the untranscendable rule of Law, described as *Yogam Aisvaram* in IX-5. It is God that works throughout all the seeming phases and complexities of life.

मया ततमिदं सर्वं जगदव्यक्तमूर्तिना ।
मत्स्थानि सर्वभूतानि न चाहं तेष्ववस्थित: ॥

All this world is pervaded by Me in form unmanifest; all beings abide in Me, but I stand apart from them.

IX-4

न च मत्स्थानि भूतानि पश्य मे योगमैश्वरम् ।
भूतभृन्न च भूतस्थो ममात्मा भूतभावन: ॥

And yet beings are not rooted in Me. Behold the scheme of My sovereignty; Myself, the origin and the support of beings, yet standing apart from them!

IX-5

प्रकृतिं स्वामवष्टभ्य विसृजामि पुनः पुनः ।
भूतग्राममिमं कृत्स्नमवशं प्रकृतेर्वशात् ॥

Using Nature, which is Mine own,
I create again and again all this
multitude of beings dependent on and
bound by nature.

IX-8

मयाऽध्यक्षेण प्रकृतिः सूयते सचराचरम् ।
हेतुनाऽनेन कौन्तेय जगद्विपरिवर्तते ॥

Under My over-seeing eye,
Nature brings forth the moving and the
unmoving and keeps the world rolling
on.

IX-10

अहं क्रतुरहं यज्ञः स्वधाऽहमहमौषधम् ।
मन्त्रोऽहमहमेवाज्यमहमग्निरहं हुतम् ॥

I am the sacrifice; I am the rite; I
am the ancestral offering; I am the
herb, the *mantra,* the butter, the fire
and the offering.

IX-16

पिताऽहमस्य जगतो माता धाता पितामहः ।
वेद्यं पवित्रमोंकार ऋक् साम यजुरेव च ॥

I am the Father of this world, the
Mother, the Supporter, the Grandsire,
the Holy One to be known, the OM, and
also the *Rik, Saman,* and *Yajus.*

IX-17

गतिर्भर्ता प्रभुः साक्षी निवासः शरणं सुहृत् ।
प्रभवः प्रलयः स्थानं निधानं बीजमव्ययम् ॥

The Path, Protector, Lord,
Witness, Abode, Asylum, Friend,
Origin, Dissolution, Foundation,
Treasure, Seed imperishable.

IX-18

तपाम्यहमहं वर्ष निगृह्णाम्युत्सृजामि च ।
अमृतं चैव मृत्युश्च सदसच्चाहमर्जुन ॥

I send heat; I hold back and pour
down the rain; I am immortality and I
am also death; I am being, and I am
also non-being.

IX-19

The following *sloka* expresses the ever
present restriction of the unchangeable law,
though within that limitation beings are free to
act:

यथाऽऽकाशस्थितो नित्यं वायुः सर्वत्रगो महान् ।
तथा सर्वाणि भूतानि मत्स्थानीत्युपधारय ॥

Reflect on this that as the mighty
air everywhere moving is yet fixed in
Space, even so all beings are dependent
on Me.

IX-6

CHAPTER IV

RIGHT ACTION

[Adhyaya II—Slokas 47, 48. Adhyaya III—
Slokas 3-9, 20, 21, 25-29, 33. Adhyaya IV—
Slokas 16, 18, 19, 22, 31-33, 37, 38, 41, 42.
Adhyaya V—Slokas 4, 7, 11. Adhyaya VI—
Slokas 1, 2. Adhyaya XVIII—Slokas 2, 7, 9,
11, 56, 57.]

WE shall now revert to the ethical teachings of
the *Bhagavad-Gita*. Reverence for the past and
the spirit of conservatism that characterize
Hindu thought should not be mistaken for
unprogressive rigidity. In spite of its undoubted
conservatism, in no other religion is there
greater elasticity, freedom of thought, or
scientific respect for truth. Hinduism has
grown and evolved like every other living body
of thought and faith. It has always displayed
the boldest varieties of conception. Various
Hindu scriptures emphasise various aspects of
the truth as the Hindu elders saw it. The *Gita*
evolves an ethic in advance not only of belief in
mere ceremonial observances, the earlier phase
of Hinduism, but also of the recluse's life of
mere abstention.

The *Gita* emphasises that the activities of
the world must go on. The good man does the
tasks to which he is called and which appertain

to his place in society. In all his activities, he does things like others outwardly; but inwardly he maintains a spirit of detachment. He does everything without selfish motive, and maintains equilibrium of mind in success and failure, pleasure and pain, joy and sorrow. Purified thus, the good man is qualified for further progress by constant meditation, prayer and devotion, and finally he "sees himself in everything and everything in God." Yoga consists in living this dedicated life in the midst of worldly affairs.

There is true renunciation in right action. What we should renounce is not action, but selfish desire. We should liberate our activities from the bondage of selfish purpose. Work should be done in a spirit of duty done, and results should not be permitted to agitate the mind. This unselfish and detached attitude can and should be cultivated even while we are engaged in life's activities. Continual practice of this attitude of mind will lead, in the higher stages of progress, to the elimination of the difference between the way of *Yoga* and the way of *Sannyasa.*

किं कर्म किमकर्मेति कवयोऽप्यत्र मोहिताः ।
तत्ते कर्म प्रवक्ष्यामि यज्ज्ञात्वा मोक्ष्यसेऽशुभात् ॥

What is action, what is inaction? Even the wise are perplexed over this. Therefore 1 shall explain to you how to act, knowing which you will be saved from evil.

IV-16

कर्मण्यकर्म यः पश्येदकर्मणि च कर्म यः ।
स बुद्धिमान्मनुष्येषु स युक्तः कृत्स्नकर्मकृत् ॥

He who perceives inaction in
action and action in inaction, has
among men attained real knowledge;
even while performing all action, he is
doing *Yoga.*

IV-18

To perceive "inaction" in "action" is to
understand and carry out the principle of
renunciation of selfish desires while doing the
work allotted to or taken up by one. To perceive
"action" in "inaction" is to realize that external
abstinence by itself does not amount to purity
of mind, and to attain by practice the control of
internal desires. This is reiterated in both
aspects in IV-41, quoted on page 46.

Activities free from selfish attachments do
not leave a *Karmic* residue.

यस्य सर्वे समारम्भाः कामसंकल्पवर्जिताः ।
ज्ञानाग्निदग्धकर्माणं तमाहुः पण्डितं बुधाः ॥

The learned deem him to have
realized the truth whose plans are not
shaped by desire and whose actions
have been purified in the furnace of
knowledge.

IV-19

यदृच्छालाभसंतुष्टो द्वन्द्वातीतो विमत्सरः ।
समः सिद्धावसिद्धौ च कृत्वाऽपि न निबध्यते ॥

Content with what comes to him
of itself, having transcended the pairs

of opposites, free from hatred, facing with equal composure success and failure, though acting he does not create bonds for himself.

IV-22

Sacrifices are prescribed in the Vedas, but, by a bold though gentle process of interpretation, the *Gita* evolves the idea that the essence of sacrifice is not ceremonial but the giving up of selfish desires. Sacrifices, the *Gita* says, may take various forms according to the true interpretation of the *Vedic* teachings. All sacrifices involve activities. This, again, is a reason why action should not be given up but just liberated from the trammels of desire and shaped into sacrifice. After thus broadening the definition of Sacrifice, the *Gita* says:

यज्ञशिष्टामृतभुजो यान्ति ब्रह्म सनातनम् ।
नायं लोकोऽस्त्ययज्ञस्य कुतोऽन्यः कुरुसत्तम ॥

The food that remains after sacrifice gives immortality. Those who eat it go to the changeless Brahma. He who does not sacrifice gains nothing even in this life; not to speak of the life beyond.

IV-31

एवं बहुविधा यज्ञा वितता ब्रह्मणो मुखे ।
कर्मजान्विद्धि तान्सर्वानेवं ज्ञात्वा विमोक्ष्यसे ॥

Many and various are the sacrifices thus spread out in the Vedas for the aspirant to choose. Know that all these come from action; knowing

this you can free yourself from
bondage.

IV-32

श्रेयान्द्रव्यमयाद्यज्ञाज्ज्ञानयज्ञ: परन्तप ।
सर्वं कर्माखिलं पार्थ ज्ञाने परिसमाप्यते ॥

Better than ritualistic sacrifice
that is performed with various articles
prescribed therefor is the sacrifice the
chief ingredient of which is right
knowledge. All prescribed actions
attain their complete fulfilment only in
true knowledge.

IV-33

Jnana (ज्ञान) manifests itself in the
cultivation of a detached attitude in all work.
Jnana is not fully expressed by "knowledge" or
"wisdom." It involves a complete transformation
of oneself in accordance with the truth that is
seen. Such transformation results from and at
the same time leads to progressive realisation
of one's unity with the rest of the world and of
the whole world with God. Action becomes free
and sinless once the motive of action is freed
from selfish aims.

This is vividly explained in the following
slokas:—

यथैधांसि समिद्धोऽग्निर्भस्मसात्कुरुतेऽर्जुन ।
ज्ञानाग्नि: सर्वकर्माणि भस्मसात्कुरुते तथा ॥

Burning fire reduces the wood to
ashes; even so does the fire of
knowledge reduce all action to ashes.

IV-37

न हि ज्ञानेन सदृशं पवित्रमिह विद्यते ।
तत्स्वयं योगसंसिद्धः कालेनात्मनि विन्दति ॥

There is no purifier in this world like knowledge; he that perfects his practice of selfless action finds that knowledge in himself in due time.

IV-38

योगसंन्यस्तकर्माणं ज्ञानसञ्छिन्नसंशयम् ।
आत्मवन्तं न कर्माणि निबध्नन्ति धनञ्जय ॥

The man who while acting yokes his action to renunciation, who has destroyed doubt by knowledge, and who is ever watchful over himself, actions do not bind.

IV-41

तस्मादज्ञानसम्भूतं हृत्स्थं ज्ञानासिनाऽऽत्मनः ।
छित्त्वैनं संशयं योगमातिष्ठोत्तिष्ठ भारत ॥

Therefore, with the sword of knowledge destroy this ignorance-born doubt that dwells in your heart, and stand up, established in *Yoga*.

IV-42

Thus, there is no real distinction between the way of renunciation and the way of duty performed. True renunciation and true performance of work are identical, the essence of both being the giving up of personal desire.

सांख्ययोगौ पृथग्बालाः प्रवदन्ति न पण्डिताः ।
एकमप्यास्थितः सम्यगुभयोर्विन्दते फलम् ॥

Children, but not those who know, speak of the *Sankhya* and the *Yoga* as different; he who is duly established in either obtains the fruits of both.

V-4

अनाश्रित: कर्मफलं कार्यं कर्म करोति य: ।
स संन्यासी च योगी च न निरग्निर्न चाक्रिय: ॥

He that performs such action as is his duty, not looking forward to the fruit of such action, is a *Sannyasi* as well as a *Yogi*, not he that gives up the household fire and sits inactive.

VI-1

यं संन्यासमिति प्राहुर्योगं तं विद्धि पाण्डव ।
न ह्यसंन्यस्तसंकल्पो योगी भवति कश्चन ॥

That which is called renunciation, know that as *Yoga*, no one can become a *Yogi* who has not renounced plans and desires.

VI-2

Once personal desire is got rid of, and the unity of all existence is realized, and, as a result thereof, the correct attitude of detachment is developed, one is an ascetic, even though engaged in all kinds of social activities.

योगयुक्तो विशुद्धात्मा विजितात्मा जितेन्द्रिय: ।
सर्वभूतात्मभूतात्मा कुर्वन्नपि न लिप्यते ॥

He is unaffected by *Karma*, although engaged in action, who has yoked himself to the way of *Yoga*, whose mind is purified, whose self has triumphed and whose senses have been subdued, and whose self has, indeed, become the self of all beings. Although acting he remains unaffected by *Karma*.

V-7

कायेन मनसा बुद्ध्या केवलैरिन्द्रियैरपि ।
योगिन: कर्म कुर्वन्ति संगं त्यक्त्वाऽऽत्मशुद्धये ॥

Yogi, having renounced attachment, performs action using the body, the mind, the reason or even the senses alone for the purpose of self-purification.

V-11

That this teaching of the *Bhagavad-Gita* is not any kind of protestant departure from Hindu doctrine but is a mere expansion of the principles enunciated by the early fathers of Hinduism is seen from the fact that all that is emphasised in the *slokas* collected in this chapter is contained in the following verses in the *Isa-vasyopanishad:*—

ईशावास्यमिदं सर्वं यत्किञ्च जगत्यां जगत् ।
तेन त्यक्तेन भुञ्जीथा मा गृध: कस्यस्विद्धनम् ॥

कुर्वन्नेवेह कर्माणि जिजीविषेच्छतं समा: ।
एवं त्वयि नान्यथेतोऽस्ति न कर्म लिप्यते नरे ॥

Everything in the universe abides in the Supreme Being. Realizing this, cast off the desires that, rise in the heart, for example, the thought of possessing what is enjoyed by another. Joy comes by that renunciation of desire. Do your work while you go through the allotted years of your life. In the detachment and dedication aforesaid lies the way for man to go uncontaminated by *Karma,* not otherwise.

The *Gita* lays reiterated emphasis on the unselfish performance of duty as preferable to attempts at renunciation of activities. The eighteenth chapter, which summarises the teachings of the *Gita,* though named *Sannyasa-Yoga,* starts with the following *slokas:*—

काम्यानां कर्मणां न्यासं संन्यासं कवयो विदुः ।
सर्वकर्मफलत्यागं प्राहुस्त्यागं विचक्षणाः ॥

Sages accept as *Sannyasa* the renouncing of works that are motived by desire. The relinquishing of the fruit of all actions is called *Tyaga* by them.

XVIII-2

नियतस्य तु संन्यासः कर्मणो नोपपद्यते ।
मोहात्तस्य परित्यागस्तामसः परिकीर्तितः ॥

Renunciation of duties that are prescribed is not proper; it is declared that such relinquishment is due to delusion and is a sign of Tamasic nature.

XVIII-7

कार्यमित्येव यत्कर्म नियतं क्रियतेऽर्जुन ।
संगं त्यक्त्वा फलं चैव स त्यागः सात्त्विको मतः ॥

The *Tyaga* that consists in the performance of prescribed duty with the feeling that it ought to be done in a spirit of detachment and not desiring for oneself the fruit thereof, is regarded as Sattvik.

XVIII-9

न हि देहभृता शक्यं त्यक्तुं कर्माण्यशेषतः ।
यस्तु कर्मफलत्यागी स त्यागीत्यभिधीयते ॥

Having to bear the burden of the physical body, one can never completely relinquish action; he who succeeds in relinquishing the fruit of action has done all and is known as *Tyagi.*

XVIII-11

This is re-stated in the following *slokas* with stress on complete surrender to the Divine and unqualified dependence on Grace:—

सर्वकर्माण्यपि सदा कुर्वाणो मद्व्यपाश्रयः ।
मत्प्रसादादवाप्नोति शाश्वतं पदमव्ययम् ॥

Though ever engaged in performing all the actions appertaining to his station, he who takes refuge in Me, by My grace attains the eternal imperishable abode.

XVIII-56

चेतसा सर्वकर्माणि मयि संन्यस्य मत्परः ।
बुद्धियोगमुपाश्रित्य मच्चित्तः सततं भव ॥

Dedicating mentally all works to Me, eager to reach Me, practise *Buddhi-Yoga,* ever filling your mind with Me.

XVIII-57

Constant contemplation of the true nature of the Soul and its relation to Matter and God is necessary for the attainment of serenity of mind. But, without the practice of a detached attitude, while performing our duties, such contemplation is not possible and can be of no avail. The practice of serenity of mind by contemplation of the Truth, and the practice of an attitude of detachment in normal activities are really complements of each other. When the effort is successful, there is no real difference between them. *Buddhi-Yoga* is attained when self-control and detachment and longing for union with God have become the normal condition of the mind.

Serenity of mind cannot come by attempting prematurely to withdraw from the world. The real merit in abstention from action lies in the absence of personal desire or motive, and this is attained in the performance of duty unaffected by personal desire. Thus *Sannyasa* and *Karma Yoga* are the same.

कर्मण्येवाधिकारस्ते मा फलेषु कदाचन ।
मा कर्मफलहेतुर्भूर्मा ते संगोऽस्त्वकर्मणि ॥

Your duty is but to act, never to be concerned with results; so let not the fruit of action be your motive. Do not let yourself be drawn into the path of non-action.

II-47

योगस्थ: कुरु कर्माणि संगं त्यक्त्वा धनञ्जय ।
सिद्ध्यसिद्ध्यो: समो भूत्वा समत्वं योग उच्यते ॥

Engage yourself in activities, established in *Yoga*, renouncing attachments, and face with even composure, success and failure. Equilibrium is called *Yoga*.

II-48

लोकेऽस्मिन्द्विविधा निष्ठा पुरा प्रोक्ता मयाऽनघ ।
ज्ञानयोगेन सांख्यानां कर्मयोगेन योगिनाम् ॥

Men can follow either of the two paths that I have revealed before, that of *Yoga* by realization of the Truth, as explained by the Sankhyas, and that of *Yoga* by unselfish and detached action, as explained by the *Yogis*.

III-3

न कर्मणामनारम्भान्नैष्कर्म्यं पुरुषोऽश्नुते ।
न च संन्यसनादेव सिद्धिं समधिगच्छति ॥

The soul does not attain freedom from action through refraining from activities. By merely abstaining, one does not attain perfection.

III-4

न हि कश्चित्क्षणमपि जातु तिष्ठत्यकर्मकृत् ।
कार्यते ह्यवशः कर्म सर्वः प्रकृतिजैर्गुणैः ॥

No one can, even for an instant, remain really actionless; for helplessly is every one propelled to action by his innate qualities.

III-5

Ambitious attempts on the part of men to retire from activity and follow the path of *Sannyasa* lead to hypocrisy and self-deception and increased impurity of mind. The safer course for men is to seek to do things in a detached spirit.

कर्मेन्द्रियाणि संयम्य य आस्ते मनसा स्मरन् ।
इन्द्रियार्थान्विमूढात्मा मिथ्याचार: स उच्यते ॥

The man who sits, restraining his organs of action, but dwelling in his mind on the objects of the senses, deludes himself and is called a hypocrite.

III-6

यस्त्विन्द्रियाणि मनसा नियम्यारभतेऽर्जुन ।
कर्मेन्द्रियै: कर्मयोगमसक्त: स विशिष्यते ॥

But he is worthy who controls the senses by his mind, uses his organs of action without developing attachment towards sense-objects, and thus practises the *Yoga* of action.

III-7

नियतं कुरु कर्म त्वं कर्म ज्यायो ह्यकर्मण: ।
शरीरयात्राऽपि च ते न प्रसिध्येदकर्मण: ॥

Engage yourself in proper activities. Action is better than non-action. Without work, even the bare sustenance of life is not possible.

III-8

यज्ञार्थात्कर्मणोऽन्यत्र लोकोऽयं कर्मबन्धनः ।
तदर्थं कर्म कौन्तेय मुक्तसंगः समाचर ॥

Men suffer the bondage of *Karma* only when an act is done otherwise than in the spirit of sacrifice. In that spirit, free from attachment, engage yourself in action.

III-9

The first impulse of a religious mind is to abstain from activity and renounce the world. Indeed, the earlier Hindu teaching displayed a leaning towards this. The *Gita,* however, definitely rejects this solution. With inherited tendencies, it emphasizes, action is inevitable. Repression causes the mind to run on, even while externally restrained from finding expression in action, and leads to hypocrisy or perversion; whereas the practice of the method of detachment trains the Soul without unnatural repression to liberate itself from the load of inherited qualities.

प्रकृतेः क्रियमाणानि गुणैः कर्माणि सर्वशः ।
अहंकारविमूढात्मा कर्ताऽहमिति मन्यते ॥

Our acts are all determined by the propensities of our nature. The illusion of the ego makes the soul consider itself the doer.

III-27

तत्त्वविच्च महाबाहो गुणकर्मविभागयोः ।
गुणा गुणेषु वर्तन्त इति मत्वा न सज्जते ॥

But he who knows the truth about propensities and action, understanding that propensities express themselves, keeps his Soul unattached.

III-28

सदृशं चेष्टते स्वस्या: प्रकृतेर्ज्ञानवानपि ।
प्रकृतिं यान्ति भूतानि निग्रह: किं करिष्यति ॥

Even the man of profound knowledge acts in conformity with his own congenital nature. All beings follow their own nature. Of what avail is suppression?

III-33

Now comes a clinching argument against leaving the world to become a recluse. You cannot set for yourself the plan of renunciation and expect others to carry on the normal work of society while you stand out. Social life must go on; and what you do, others must be expected to copy. The ethic of the *Gita* is pre-eminently a social one. What was good for great Janaka, it says, is good enough for all.

कर्मणैव हि संसिद्धिमास्थिता जनकादय: ।
लोकसंग्रहमेवापि सम्पश्यन्-कर्तुमर्हसि ॥

Janaka and others attained perfection only through performance of duties. Looking even to the welfare of society, you should work.

III-20

यद्यदाचरति श्रेष्ठस्तत्तदेवेतरो जनः ।
स यत्प्रमाणं कुरुते लोकस्तदनुवर्तते ॥

Whatever way of life a high-
placed man adopts, other men copy;
the standard he sets up is followed by
the people.

III-21

The co-operation of all is needed for the
world—of the wise as well as of the ignorant.
The ranks of the wise may and should steadily
increase. But it should not be forgotten
meanwhile that social life cannot dispense with
the co-operation of the ignorant. Their minds,
therefore, should not be purposely disturbed.

सक्ताः कर्मण्याविद्वांसो यथा कुर्वन्ति भारत ।
कुर्याद्विद्वांस्तथाऽसक्तश्चिकीर्षुर्लोकसंग्रहम् ॥

The informed should toil with the
motive of the social welfare without
attachment, even as the uninformed
toil, moved by personal desire for
results.

III-25

न बुद्धिभेदं जनयेदज्ञानां कर्मसंगिनाम् ।
जोषयेत्सर्वकर्माणि विद्वान्युक्तः समाचरन् ॥

Let no man who has the
advantage of knowledge unsettle the
mind of ignorant people who are moved
by attachment to the results of action;
but, himself following the rule of *Yoga*,
let him work rendering all action
attractive.

III-26

प्रकृतेर्गुणसम्मूढाः सज्जन्ते गुणकर्मसु ।
तानकृत्स्नविदो मन्दान्कृत्स्नविन्न विचालयेत् ॥

Those on whom the qualities of matter have wrought their spell are propelled to action by the attachments so generated. The man who has realized the truth should not unsettle the imperfect understanding of the weak-minded.

III-29

Chapter V

THE PRACTICE OF MIND-CONTROL

[Adhyaya II—Slokas 60-63, 67. Adhyaya III—
Slokas 36-41. Adhyaya XVI—Slokas 21, 22.
Adhyaya XVIII—Slokas 36, 37]

THE *Gita* teaching explained in the previous chapter, *viz.* that true renunciation is best exhibited in selfless performance of work and not in withdrawal from the world, is not a theory put forward to serve as a defence or an apology for those who are unwilling to withdraw from the world. It is intended to be the basis for the actual moulding of men's lives, so as to develop a habitual and spontaneous attitude of selflessness and detachment. As a duck swims in water and when it steps out sheds the water from off its back, so should we learn to move in the world; not wanting in expertness or tidiness· or efficiency in work, but vigilantly guarding against the development of selfish attachments. Constant practice of control of mind is essential to enable one to maintain this detached attitude.

The enemies of good resolution are lust, anger and greed. He who wishes to develop detachment must be continually on the watch against these perturbations of the mind. If the mind is controlled, the rest will take care of itself. The power of thought is great, for either good or evil. If the mind is not carefully guarded, desire will find its perch in the senses, seize our thoughts, pollute our intelligence and finally ruin us. Therefore the battle must be fought with desire at the gate, even while it seeks entrance in our thoughts.

यततो ह्यपि कौन्तेय पुरुषस्य विपश्चितः ।
इन्द्रियाणि प्रमाथीनि हरन्ति प्रसभं मनः ॥

The rebellious nature of the senses is such that even in a man who knows and who is sincerely striving they are apt violently to carry away his mind.

II-60

तानि सर्वाणि संयम्य युक्त आसीत मत्परः ।
वशे हि यस्येन्द्रियाणि तस्य प्रज्ञा प्रतिष्ठिता ॥

Restraining them all, he should sit with his mind composed and bent on Me. He whose senses are mastered has his understanding firmly fixed.

II-61

ध्यायतो विषयान्पुंसः संगस्तेषूपजायते ।
संगात्सञ्जायते कामः कामात्क्रोधोऽभिजायते ॥

When a man allows his mind to muse on the objects of sense-enjoyments, an attraction for them is created. Attraction develops into craving, and from craving follow causes for anger.

II-62

क्रोधाद्भवति सम्मोह: सम्मोहात्स्मृतिविभ्रम: ।
स्मृतिभ्रंशाद्बुद्धिनाशो बुद्धिनाशात्प्रणश्यति ॥

Anger produces delusion.
Delusion confuses the memory and
understanding of things; from this
confusion of understanding follows the
disintegration of the power of
discrimination; with discrimination
gone, the man perishes.

II-63

इन्द्रियाणां हि चरतां यन्मनोऽनु विधीयते ।
तदस्य हरति प्रज्ञां वायुर्नावमिवाम्भसि ॥

The mind that follows the
wandering senses carries away the
Reason of the man with it, as the gale
bears away the ship on the ocean.

II-67

अर्जुन उवाच

अथ केन प्रयुक्तोऽयं पापं चरति पूरुष: ।
अनिच्छन्नपि वार्ष्णेय बलादिव नियोजित: ॥

Arjuna asked:

But impelled by what, does a
man commit sin, as it were by force
constrained, though he does not wish,
indeed, to be a sinful man?

III-36

श्रीभगवानुवाच

काम एष क्रोध एष रजोगुणसमुद्भव: ।
महाशनो महापाप्मा विद्ध्येनमिह वैरिणम् ॥

The Lord said:

It is desire. It is anger. It is born out of the principle of passion in nature, insatiable and all-polluting. Know it as our enemy here on earth.

III-37

धूमेनाव्रियते वह्निर्यथाऽऽदर्शो मलेन च ।
यथोल्बेनावृतो गर्भस्तथा तेनेदमावृतम् ॥

As smoke surrounds fire, as a mirror is covered over with dust, as the embryo is encased in the womb, the understanding is enveloped by this enemy.

III-38

आवृतं ज्ञानमेतेन ज्ञानिनो नित्यवैरिणा ।
कामरूपेण कौन्तेय दुष्पूरेणानलेन च ॥

This perpetual enemy of the wise, this unquenchable and insatiable foe, Desire, surrounds and holds the understanding as prisoner.

III-39

इन्द्रियाणि मनो बुद्धिरस्याधिष्ठानमुच्यते ।
एतैर्विमोहयत्येष ज्ञानमावृत्य देहिनम् ॥

It is said that this enemy seizing the senses, the mind and Reason and thus closely surrounding and isolating the understanding, uses them to bewilder the soul

III-40

तस्मात्त्वमिन्द्रियाण्यादौ नियम्य भरतर्षभ ।
पाप्मानं प्रजहि ह्येनं ज्ञानविज्ञाननाशनम् ॥

Therefore, governing first the senses, slay this evil thing, which otherwise will destroy knowledge and discrimination.

III-41

त्रिविधं नरकस्येदं द्वारं नाशनमात्मनः ।
कामः क्रोधस्तथा लोभस्तस्मादेत्त्रयं त्यजेत् ॥

There are three gateways to hell, by which one's self-ruin is brought about—lust, anger and greed; therefore let these three be renounced.

XVI-21

एतैर्विमुक्तः कौन्तेय तमोद्वारैस्त्रिभिर्नरः ।
आचरत्यात्मनः श्रेयस्ततो याति परां गतिम् ॥

Saved from these three gates of darkness, man works out the good of his self, and reaches the highest goal.

XVI-22

True happiness does not come from that which at first is like nectar, but which in the end becomes, indeed, venom. Self-control leads to true happiness, though in the beginning it is hard and bitter.

सुखं त्विदानीं त्रिविधं शृणु मे भरतर्षभ ।
अभ्यासाद्रमते यत्र दुःखान्तं च निगच्छति ॥
यत्तदग्रे विषमिव परिणामेऽमृतोपमम् ।
तत्सुखं सात्त्विकं प्रोक्तमात्मबुद्धिप्रसादजम् ॥

Of three kinds of pleasure, that in which one by gradual practice rejoices and in which one finds an end to grief, which at first is as venom, distasteful, but in the end is like nectar; that pleasure is said to be Sattvik, born of the clarified understanding of the soul.

XVIII-36, 37

CHAPTER VI

MEDITATION

[Adhyaya II—Slokas 14, 15, 38. Adhyaya V-
Slokas 22-24, 26, 28 Adhyaya VI—Slokas 3-7,
10-14, 16, 17, 19, 24-27. Adhyaya XII—
Slokas 13-19. Adhyaya XIV—Slokas 22-25.]

AFTER practising an attitude of unselfishness
when engaged in normal activities, the aspirant
can advance towards an attitude of indifference
to pain and pleasure. Success or failure in any
endeavour should not agitate the mind. Pain
and pleasure should be welcomed with
equanimity as being impermanent and, in the
very nature of things, complementary to each
other. They are part of the universal law of
relativity, inescapable. They arise out of the
"contacts of matter" and have no effect on the
soul.

मात्रास्पर्शास्तु कौन्तेय शीतोष्णसुखदुःखदाः ।
आगमापायिनोऽनित्यास्तांस्तितिक्षस्व भारत ॥

Material contact produces cold
and heat, pleasure and pain. These
sensations are fleeting and
insubstantial; go through them
unruffled.

II-14

यं हि न व्यथयन्त्येते पुरुषं पुरुषर्षभ ।
समदुःखसुखं धीरं सोऽमृतत्वाय कल्पते ॥

The man who is not ruffled by
these, who is brave, and the same in
pain and pleasure, shapes himself for
immortality.

II-15

सुखदुःखे समे कृत्वा लाभालाभौ जयाजयौ ।
ततो युद्धाय युज्यस्व नैवं पापमवाप्स्यसि ॥

Welcoming, with equanimity,
pleasure and pain, acquisitions and
losses, victory and defeat, get ready for
battle; thus you shall not incur sin.

II-38

It is one's own thoughts and one's own
actions that affect the fortunes of one's soul,
not the alternating joy or sorrow that comes
from without.

True happiness comes not from contact-
born pleasures, but from self-control. The
serenity of mind that is attained by the practice
of self-control works such a change that it may
be said that thereby the soul is liberated even
though it is still imprisoned in the flesh.

ये हि संस्पर्शजा भोगा दुःखयोनय एव ते ।
आद्यन्तवन्तः कौन्तेय न तेषु रमते बुधः ॥

The pleasures that are contact-
born become, indeed, wombs of pain.
Such pleasures have beginning and
ending; the wise do not rejoice in them.

V-22

शक्नोतीहैव यः सोढुं प्राक् शरीरविमोक्षणात् ।
कामक्रोधोद्भवं वेगं स युक्तः स सुखी नरः ॥

He is a happy man and a *Yogi*
who learns to withstand here on earth,
ere he be liberated from the body, the
force of desire and anger.

V-23

योऽन्तः सुखोऽन्तरारामस्तथान्तज्र्योतिरेव यः ।
स योगी ब्रह्मनिर्वाणं ब्रह्मभूतोऽधिगच्छति ॥

He whose pleasure is within
himself, who derives joy within himself,
who has a shining light within himself,
that *Yogi* attains final liberation and is
absorbed in Brahma.

V-24

कामक्रोधवियुक्तानां यतीनां यतचेतसाम् ।
अभितो ब्रह्मनिर्वाणं वर्तते विदितात्मनाम् ॥

Final liberation lies near to those
seekers who control their mind, who
cast off desire and passion and who
know themselves.

V-26

यतेन्द्रियमनोबुद्धिर्मुनिर्मोक्षपरायणः ।
विगतेच्छाभयक्रोधो यः सदा मुक्त एव सः ॥

With senses, mind and intellect
ever under control, absorbed in the
pursuit of final liberation, the sage, free
from desire, fear and anger, is, indeed,
already liberated.

V-28

It would, however, be premature to attempt to attain this serenity of mind without first habituating oneself to unselfish performance of all duties. If the unselfish attitude is by practice made almost spontaneous in normal activities, one is qualified to enter on the more difficult practice of serenity irrespective of success or failure, or of joy or sorrow.

आरुरुक्षोर्मुनेर्योगं कर्म कारणमुच्यते ।
योगारूढस्य तस्यैव शम: कारणमुच्यते ॥

For a sage who is seeking *Yoga*, performance of duty is declared to be the means; when he is well confirmed in the practice of *Yoga*, serenity is declared the means.

VI-3

यदा हि नेन्द्रियार्थेषु न कर्मस्वनुषज्जते ।
सर्वसंकल्पसंन्यासी योगारूढस्तदोच्यते ॥

When a man feels no craving for the objects of sense or for being engaged in activities therefor, and his mind is free of all such plans of action, then he is said to be confirmed in the practice of *Yoga*.

VI-4

उद्धरेदात्मनाऽऽत्मानं नात्मानमवसादयेत् ।
आत्मैव ह्यात्मनो बन्धुरात्मैव रिपुरात्मन: ॥

Let one raise the Self by the Self and not let the Self within become weak; the Self is, indeed, the Self's only

friend, but the Self is also its own
enemy.

VI-5

बन्धुरात्माऽऽत्मनस्तस्य येनात्मैवात्मना जितः ।
अनात्मनस्तु शत्रुत्वे वर्तेतात्मैव शत्रुवत् ॥

He who has conquered himself
by self-control finds a friend in himself;
but he becomes verily his own worst
enemy if he has not learnt to govern
himself.

VI-6

जितात्मनः प्रशान्तस्य परमात्मा समाहितः ।
शीतोष्णसुखदुःखेषु तथा मानापमानयोः ॥

The transfigured Self of him who
has attained self-control and
equanimity is unruffled in cold and
heat, pleasure and pain, honour and
disgrace.

VI-7

After one has trained oneself to be a
Karma-yogin, that is to say, to do the duties
that fall to one's lot without selfish desire and
without agitation as to success or failure, one
is advised as often as possible to withdraw from
the world for deep and undisturbed meditation.
Such meditation is a great aid to secure
serenity of mind. *Yoga* in the following slokas is
the practice of such meditation:—

योगी युञ्जीत सततमात्मानं रहसि स्थितः ।
एकाकी यतचित्तात्मा निराशीरपरिग्रहः ॥

Let the *Yogi* often retire to a secluded place, alone, with mind controlled, and divesting himself of wishes and of all thought as to possessions, and concentrate his mind on his soul.

VI-10

शुचौ देशे प्रतिष्ठाप्य स्थिरमासनमात्मनः ।
नात्युच्छ्रितं नातिनीचं चैलाजिनकुशोत्तरम् ॥

Seated in a clean place, on a fixed seat prepared for himself, neither very much raised nor very low, covered over with cloth, skin and Kusha grass.

VI-11

तत्रैकाग्रं मनः कृत्वा यतचित्तेन्द्रियक्रियः ।
उपविश्यासने युञ्ज्याद्योगमात्मविशुद्धये ॥

There, having steadied his mind, controlling thought and the functions of the senses, sitting on his seat, he should engage himself in meditation for the purification of the Self.

VI-12

समं कायशिरोग्रीवं धारयन्नचलं स्थिरः ।
संप्रेक्ष्य नासिकाग्रं स्वं दिशश्चानवलोकयन् ॥

With body, head and neck erect, not shaking, steady, eyes turned to the point of the nose and gaze not wandering.

VI-13

प्रशान्तात्मा विगतभीर्ब्रह्मचारिव्रते स्थितः ।
मनः संयम्य मच्चितो युक्त आसीत मत्परः ॥

With internal calm, fearless, firm
in the vow of Brahmacharya, the mind
well governed, thinking of Me, let him
sit harmonised and absorbed in
attaining Me.

VI-14

नात्यश्नतस्तु योगोऽस्ति न चैकान्तमनश्नतः ।
न चातिस्वप्नशीलस्य जाग्रतो नैव चार्जुन ॥

Yoga is not for him who eats too
much, nor for one who absolutely
abstains from food; it is not for him
who is too much addicted to sleep, nor
is it to be attained by keeping vigils.

VI-16

युक्ताहारविहारस्य युक्तचेष्टस्य कर्मसु ।
युक्तस्वप्नावबोधस्य योगो भवति दुःखहा ॥

Yoga, the destroyer of pain, is for
him whose food, diversions, work, sleep
and waking are all controlled and
regulated.

VI-17

यथा दीपो निवातस्थो नेङ्गते सोपमा स्मृता ।
योगिनो यतचितस्य युञ्जतो योगमात्मनः ॥

When a lamp is set in a place
where the air is absolutely still, the
flame does not flicker. To this is likened
the steadfast meditation of the *Yogi*,
whose mind is under control.

VI-19

Note the insistence on moderation in everything including austerities. The secret of success is in steady practice in the art of controlling thoughts which continually seek to run away with the mind; and not in excessive severity of austerities.

संकल्पप्रभवान्कामांस्त्यक्त्वा सर्वानशेषतः ।
मनसैवेन्द्रियग्रामं विनियम्य समन्ततः ॥

Keeping the mind absolutely free from all desires and using the mind to curb the senses, in every direction.

VI-24

शनैःशनैरुपरमेद् बुद्ध्या धृतिगृहीतया ।
आत्मसंस्थं मनः कृत्वा न किञ्चिदपि चिन्तयेत् ॥

Let him use his *Buddhi* with steady application gradually to withdraw into himself and thus having made the mind abide in the Self, let him not think of anything.

VI-25

यतो यतो निस्सरति मनश्चञ्चलमस्थिरम् ।
ततस्ततो नियम्यैतदात्मन्येव वशं नयेत् ॥

Each time the wavering and unsteady mind seeks to wander, let him restrain and bring it under control and lead it to abide in the Self.

VI-26

प्रशान्तमनसं ह्येनं योगिनं सुखमुत्तमम् ।
उपैति शान्तरजसं ब्रह्मभूतमकल्मषम् ॥

The purest joy comes to the *Yogin* who has quelled the restlessness within him, whose mind has attained calm, and who, thus purified, has attained his true self and turned himself to the Infinite.

VI-27

The following *slokas* in the 12th *Adhyaya* describe the man who has attained this ideal serenity of mind:—

अद्वेष्टा सर्वभूतानां मैत्र: करुण एव च ।
निर्ममो निरहंकार: समदु:खसुख: क्षमी ॥

He who has no hatred, and is a friend of all living things, full of compassion, without the feeling of "I" or "Mine," balanced in pleasure and pain, and ever forbearing.

XII-13

सन्तुष्ट: सततं योगी यतात्मा दृढनिश्चय: ।
मय्यर्पितमनोबुद्धिर्यो मे भक्त: स मे प्रिय: ॥

Content always and yoked to the Spirit, self-controlled, resolute, with emotion and understanding dedicated to Me, he is My devotee, and is dear to Me.

XII-14

यस्मान्नोद्विजते लोको लोकान्नोद्विजते च य: ।
हर्षामर्षभयोद्वेगैर्मुक्तो य: स च मे प्रिय: ॥

He who does not cause perturbation to other beings, and who is himself not perturbed at the world,

who is free from the agitation of joy,
anger and fear, he is dear to Me.

XII-15

अनपेक्ष: शुचिर्दक्ष उदासीनो गतव्यथ: ।
सर्वारम्भपरित्यागी यो मद्भक्त: स मे प्रिय: ॥

He who desires nothing, is pure,
right-minded, passionless, unruffled,
has renounced all worldly plans, he,
My devotee, is dear to Me.

XII-16

यो न हृष्यति न द्वेष्टि न शोचति न कांक्षति ।
शुभाशुभपरित्यागी भक्तिमान्य: स मे प्रिय: ॥

He who does not live or hate, who
does not grieve or long for anything,
who has given up looking on things as
welcome and unwelcome, such a
devotee is dear to Me.

XII-17

सम: शत्रौ च मित्रे च तथा मानापमानयो: ।
शीतोष्णसुखदु:खेषु सम: संगविवर्जित: ॥

Alike in mind to those who are
friendly to him or unfriendly, and
looking with even composure on fame
and obloquy, alike in cold and heat,
pleasure and pain, free from
attachments.

XII-18

तुल्यनिन्दास्तुतिर्मौनी संतुष्टो येन केनचित् ।
अनिकेत: स्थिरमतिर्भक्तिमान्मे प्रियो नर: ॥

Valuing praise and reproach
alike, silent, wholly content with what
comes, not looking on any place as his
home, firm in mind, he is My devotee
and such a one is dear to Me.

XII-19

The serenity of mind thus developed by
the regulation of activities and regular
meditation is ever liable to be disturbed by the
forces of the inherited physical body. These
tend to operate in spite of self-realization, but
the wise man protects himself by continually
reminding himself of the truth. He is not
agitated by the changing phases of his nature,
which now may be equilibrium, and now urge
for action, or again inertia.

प्रकाशं च प्रवृत्तिं च मोहमेव च पाण्डव ।
न द्वेष्टि संप्रवृत्तानि न निवृत्तानि कांक्षति ॥

He who welcomes clarity of spirit,
the urge to activity, and even delusion
as they come, but does not long for
them again when they disappear.

XIV-22

उदासीनवदासीनो गुणैर्यो न विचाल्यते ।
गुणा वर्तन्त इत्येव योऽवतिष्ठति नेङ्गते ॥

He who remains unmoved,
keeping his inner spirit unaffected and
unruffled by the changing moods,
saying to himself, "The qualities of my
material body are just moving."

XIV-23

समदुःखसुखः स्वस्थः समलोष्टाश्मकाञ्चनः ।
तुल्यप्रियाप्रियो धीरस्तुल्यनिन्दात्मसंस्तुतिः ॥

Equally welcoming pain and pleasure, self-sustained and brave, to whom a clod of earth, a piece of stone and a nugget of gold are just the same, who makes no difference between those that are dear and those who are not and is the same in praise or blame.

XIV-24

मानापमानयोस्तुल्यस्तुल्यो मित्रारिपक्षयोः ।
सर्वारम्भपरित्यागी गुणातीतः स उच्यते ॥

The same in honour and calumny, the same to friend and foe; having abandoned all worldly undertaking—such a one is declared as having overcome natural propensities.

XIV-25

CHAPTER VII

INHERITED PROPENSITIES

[Adhyaya V—Slokas 14, 15. Adhyaya XIII—
Slokas 29-31. Adhyaya XIV—Slokas 5, 19.
Adhyaya XVIII—Slokas 40, 60, 61.]

AS an aid to charity in judging others and to serve to calm the mind in moments of agitation, it is very useful to remember why men act wrongly. There is a load of congenital qualities with which we begin and which tend to find expression whenever we fail to exercise self-control. We should think of our own weaknesses when we see others fail. Again, behind everything is God, the real Actor. We should not be disturbed by the constant appearance of what seems to our limited understanding to be evil. His will and His plans are inscrutable, though worked through natural laws.

न कर्तृत्त्वं न कर्माणि लोकस्य सृजति प्रभु: ।
न कर्मफलसंयोगं स्वभावस्तु प्रवर्तते ॥

The soul does not exercise any agency or perform action, nor is it concerned with the fruits of action. It is the qualities of material nature that carry on,

नादत्ते कस्यचित्पापं न चैव सुकृतं विभुः ।
अज्ञानेनावृतं ज्ञानं तेन मुह्यन्ति जन्तवः ॥

The soul in its true nature is unaffected by evil-doing in any, or by kindness either. True understanding is darkened by ignorance, thereby are creatures deluded.

V-15

प्रकृत्यैव च कर्माणि क्रियमाणानि सर्वशः ।
यः पश्यति तथाऽऽत्मानमकर्तारं स पश्यति ॥

He sees the truth who perceives that the forces of material nature really bring about all actions, and that the Self is actionless.

XIII-29

यदा भूतपृथग्भावमेकस्थमनुपश्यति ।
तत एव च विस्तारं ब्रह्म संपद्यते तदा ॥

When one perceives the common basis of all diversified existence and how everything shapes itself and spreads out from it, one realizes Brahma.

XIII-30

अनादित्वान्निर्गुणत्वात्परमात्माऽयमव्ययः ।
शरीरस्थोऽपि कौन्तेय न करोति न लिप्यते ॥

Being beginningless and without material qualities, the immutable and pure soul, though seated in the body, neither acts nor is affected.

XIII-31

सत्त्वं रजस्तम इति गुणाः प्रकृतिसम्भवाः ।
निबध्नन्ति महाबाहो देहे देहिनमव्ययम् ॥

Goodness, the spirit of activity
and inertia are the principles that move
men; they are matter-born; while in the
body the soul, though itself immutable,
is tied up to and moved by those
qualities.

XIV-5

नान्यं गुणेभ्यः कर्तारं यदा द्रष्टाऽनुपश्यति ।
गुणेभ्यश्च परं वेत्ति मद्भावं सोऽधिगच्छति ॥

That man has attained My spirit
who has realised that there is no
agency other than the qualities of
material nature, and who has seen that
which stands higher than these
qualities.

XIV-19

न तदस्ति पृथिव्यां वा दिवि देवेषु वा पुनः ।
सत्त्वं प्रकृतिजैर्मुक्तं यदेभिः स्यात् त्रिभिर्गुणैः ॥

There is no being on earth or even
in heaven among the gods that is
liberated from these three qualities
born of matter.

XVIII-40

स्वभावजेन कौन्तेय निबद्धः स्वेन कर्मणा ।
कर्तुं नेच्छसि यन्मोहात् करिष्यस्यवशोऽपि तत् ॥

That which you desire to abstain
from through false notions, even that

you will helplessly do, impelled by the motion of your own nature.

XVIII-60

ईश्वरः सर्वभूतानां हृद्देशेऽर्जुन तिष्ठति ।
भ्रामयन् सर्वभूतानि यन्त्रारूढानि मायया ॥

The Lord dwells in the hearts of all beings, and through the forces of *Maya* causes all beings to move like puppets on a revolving machine.

XVIII-61

Maya is here material nature constituted by the *Gunas*. The lesson of the above *slokas* is that the qualities with which men start on their life journeys determine their activities. We should not be moved to anger or contempt if any one commits what we deem to be wrong, nor pride ourselves upon our own good actions. The *slokas* are not to be interpreted as if men were absolved from responsibility. The *Gita* makes it clear that it is only by personal effort and by the practice of self-control that we may be delivered of the character-load with which we begin. That men are moved by congenital qualities born of previous *Karma*, which defeat all efforts at ignoring them, is a teaching to cultivate charity towards others and serenity in ourselves, and not a doctrine of irresponsibility. It would be the reverse of what the *Gita* teaches if the inevitability of qualities resulting from *Karma* moves us to contempt or cruelty towards others, instead of making us more charitable.

The self is, in one sense, not the real actor, but in another sense he is. The *Gunas* have their roots in the body, lead the physical senses and the body, and hold the Spirit within as a prisoner. The Spirit, however, can detach itself and overcome the qualities. For this, however, *Jnana* (ज्ञान) is essential. *Jnana* is not a thing to be attained by mere study or meditation. It can be attained in a real and useful sense only by self-control in thought and action. The tendencies of men broadly classified as सत्व, रजस् and तमस् *(Sattva, Rajas and Tamas)* are matter-born and matter-bound, i.e., have their origin and sustenance in the *Prakriti* which embodies the soul, But they have their resultant effect on the soul. By the exercise of self-control and true knowledge, a man can realize his own freedom, irrespective of these inherited qualities and principles of material nature. If he does not exercise self-control and practise an attitude of detachment, he will not only remain bound unto this load, but increase it.

CHAPTER VIII

HOPE FOR ALL

[Adhyaya IV—Sloka 11. Adhyaya VII—
Slokas 20-22. Adhyaya IX—Slokas 23, 26,
27; 29-31.]

THE doctrine of *Karma* should not frighten us. Law is immutable but God is Love as well as Law. There is none who need despair on the ground that his sins have been too great or too many. Prayer and repentance purify the soul. According to the *Gita*, whatever might have been said in the Hindu codes of observances, neither sex nor caste makes any difference in the way of Grace.

समोऽहं सर्वभूतेषु न मे द्वेष्योऽस्ति न प्रिय: ।
ये भजन्ति तु मां भक्त्या मयि ते तेषु चाप्यहम् ॥

The same am I to all beings; there is none hateful to Me, nor dear. They who worship Me with devotion are in Me, and so am I in them.

IX-29

अपि चेत्सुदुराचारो भजते मामनन्यभाक् ।
साधुरेव स मन्तव्य: सम्यग् व्यवसितो हि स: ॥

If even he who has greatly erred turns to Me with single-minded devotion, he too must be counted among the good, for he has resolved well.

IX-30

क्षिप्रं भवति धर्मात्मा शश्वच्छान्तिं निगच्छति ।
कौन्तेय प्रतिजानीहि न मे भक्त: प्रणश्यति ॥

Soon he becomes purified in spirit and attains abiding peace; know for certain that he who gives Me his devotion can never be lost.

IX-31

And particularly referring to caste and sex disqualifications:

मां हि पार्थ व्यपाश्रित्य येऽपि स्यु: पापयोनय: ।
स्त्रियो वैश्यास्तया शूद्रास्तेऽपि यान्ति परां गतिम् ॥

They who seek refuge in Me, though born in the lowest condition, and be they women or Vaishyas or Sudras, they also attain the highest abode.

IX-32

Genuine prayer and repentance are counter-motions in the field of *Karma* and neutralise previous acts. But no one may deliberately indulge in sin on the assurance that the sin may later be washed away. True repentance, which alone can be of avail, does not come that way. Genuine penitence is a motion of the mind involving intense pain and is itself a self-imposed punishment, neutralizer and a corrective for past sins, but it so acts only in the measure that it is truly suffered.

Repentance and self-abasement and prayers for grace and mercy are operations of the mind, not words or ceremonies gone through or absolution procured from priests. Words and ceremonies and priests may be helpful through inspiring association, and as aids to focus the mind in penitent thought, but are not in themselves cleansers of sin. A man may deceive himself or others, but he cannot deceive Truth itself. And *Karma* is immutable Truth. You may mislead the patient about his temperature or deceive your customer about the weights of things sold to him, but you cannot cheat the thermometer or the scales themselves.

Forms of worship do not matter. They may vary, but are all in reality one. This is the great, all-important and unique attitude of Hinduism towards the so-called religious differences.

ये यथा मां प्रपद्यन्ते तांस्तथैव भजाम्यहम् ।
मम वर्त्मानुवर्तन्ते मनुष्या: पार्थ सर्वश: ॥

In whatsoever way men approach
Me, even so do I bless them, for
whatever the paths that men may take
in worship, they come unto Me.

IV-11

When we consider how long ago this truth was seen and laid down for men's guidance in such emphatic terms, we are in a position to appreciate and admire the spiritual greatness of the fathers of Hinduism.

येऽप्यन्यदेवता भक्ता यजन्ते श्रद्धयाऽन्विताः ।
तेऽपि मामेव कौन्तेय यजन्त्यविधिपूर्वकम् ॥

Even the devotees of other gods who worship them full of faith, even they worship but Me, though irregularly.

IX-23

पत्रं पुष्पं फलं तोयं तो मे भक्त्या प्रयच्छति ।
तदहं भक्त्युपहृतमश्नामि प्रयतात्मनः ॥

Whatever is offered to Me with devotion, be it a leaf, a flower, a fruit or water, is eagerly accepted by Me as the devoted offering of a striving soul.

IX-26

यत्करोषि यदश्नासि यज्जुहोषि ददासि यत् ।
यत्तपस्यसि कौन्तेय तत्कुरुष्व मदर्पणम् ॥

Whatsoever you do, whatsoever, you eat, whatsoever you offer in sacrifice, whatsoever alms you give, whatsoever penance you undergo, do it as an offering unto Me.

IX-27

कामैस्तैस्तैर्हृतज्ञानाः प्रपद्यन्तेऽन्यदेवताः ।
तं तं नियममास्थाय प्रकृत्या नियताः स्वया ॥

They whose understanding has been seized by various desires go to other gods, resorting to various external observances, conforming to their own natures.

VII-20

यो यो यां यां तनुं भक्त: श्रद्धयार्चितुमिच्छति ।
तस्य तस्याचलां श्रद्धां तामेव विदधाम्यहम् ॥

Whosoever the devotee and
whatsoever the form worshipped with
sincere faith, it is I who bestow on him
that firm faith.

VII-21

स तया श्रद्धया युक्तस्तस्याराधनमीहते ।
लभते च तत: कामान्मयैव विहितान्हि तान् ॥

He, filled with that faith, seeks
to worship such form. He obtains his
desires, I verily decreeing them.

VII-22

This teaching, of course, referred to the
unity of goal of all forms of worship that were
prevalent at the time. We may not claim that
the varieties of religions and religious practices
that came into existence much later were then
thought of. But the doctrine is stated in such
wide terms and so broad-based on essential
principle as to be applicable to every variety of
religion.

CHAPTER IX

GODLESSNESS

[Adhyaya XVI—Slokas 7-18, 23, 24.]

WHILE it is true that whatever may be the form of worship God is reached, the *Gita* condemns godlessness and materialism in no uncertain terms, describing the materialist code of life in language that seems almost to refer to present-day affairs.

The materialist does not admit that there is anything in itself right or wrong.

प्रवृत्तिं च निवृत्तिं च जना न विदुरासुराः ।
न शौचं नापि चाचारो न सत्यं तेषु विद्यते ॥

Men born with evil tendency know neither what is right to do to achieve a good object, nor what is right to abstain from doing to avert evil; neither purity nor truth, nor even right behaviour is found in them.

XVI-7

The materialist theory of life is stated thus:

अस्तयमप्रतिष्ठं ते जगदाहुरनीश्वरम् ।
अपरस्परसम्भूतं किमन्यत्कामहैतुकम् ॥

The universe is not based on truth; it is not supported by any

spiritual law; it is not ruled by God;
life is brought about by the coming
together of matter, by the attraction of
desire, and nothing else; thus these
men aver.

XVI-8

Godlessness leads to false ideas of
progress and civilisation, exploitation and war.

एतां दृष्टिमवष्टभ्य नष्टात्मानोऽल्पबुद्धयः ।
प्रभवन्त्युग्रकर्माणः क्षयाय जगतोऽहिताः ॥

Holding this view of life, these
conscienceless men of small
understanding undertake fierce deeds
and become enemies of the world and
lead it to destruction.

XVI-9

काममाश्रित्यं दुष्पूरं दम्भमानमदान्विताः ।
मोहाद्गृहीत्वाऽसद्ग्राहान्प्रवर्तन्तेऽशुचिव्रताः ॥

Seeking to fulfil insatiable
desires, moved by vanity, self-conceit
and pride, holding to evil ideas
obstinately through delusion, they
engage themselves in action with
impure resolves.

XVI-10

चिन्तामपरिमेयां च प्रलयान्तामुपाश्रिताः ।
कामोपभोगपरमा एतावदिति निश्चिताः ॥

Giving themselves over to
unnumbered cares until death,
regarding the gratification of desires as
the highest object, believing firmly that
there is nought else in the world.

XVI-11

आशापाशशतैर्बद्धा: कामक्रोधपरायणा: ।
ईहन्ते कामभोगार्थमन्यायेनार्थ संचयान् ॥

Held in bondage by a hundred
cords of hopes and expectations, given
over to lust and anger, they seek by
unlawful means to hoard wealth for
gratification of sensual desires.

XVI-12

The pride of power and possession, be it
of the individual, the group or the nation, and
the destruction and anarchy which it leads to
are described below:

इदमद्य मया लब्धमिमं प्राप्स्ये मनोरथम् ।
इदमस्तीदमपि मे भविष्यति पुनर्धनम् ॥

"This has been acquired by me
today, this purpose I shall gain; this
wealth is mine, and this also shall be
mine soon."

XVI-13

असौ मया हत: शत्रुर्हनिष्ये चापरानपि ।
ईश्वरोऽहमहं भोगी सिद्धोऽहं बलवान्सुखी ॥

"I have destroyed this enemy,
and others also I shall slay. I rule, I
command pleasures, I am successful,
I am strong, I am born to be happy."

XVI-14

आढ्योऽभिजनवानस्मि कोऽन्योऽस्ति सदृशो मया ।
यक्ष्ये दास्यामि मोदिष्य इत्यज्ञानविमोहिता: ॥

"I am wealthy, well-born; who
else is there that is like me? I will
perform sacrifices, I will give alms, I
will enjoy." Thus deluded by ignorance.

XVI-15

अनेकचित्तविभ्रान्ता मोहजालसमावृताः ।
प्रसक्ताः कामभोगेषु पतन्ति नरकेऽशुचौ ॥

Agitated by numerous thoughts,
enmeshed in the net of delusion, and
addicted to the gratification of desire,
they fall into foul hell.

XVI-16

Pride of race and the vain glory of so-
called culture or civilization, or even
philanthropy cannot save them from the end to
which the sins on which it is all founded must
take them.

आत्मसंभाविताः स्तब्धा धनमानमदान्विताः ।
यजन्ते नामयज्ञैस्ते दम्भेनाविधिपूर्बबम् ॥

Vain, stubborn, intoxicated by
wealth and pride, they go in name
through the performance of sacrifices
for ostentation, contrary to rule.

XVI-17

अहंकारं बलं दर्पं कामं क्रोधं च संश्रिताः ।
मामात्मपरदेहेषु प्रद्विषन्तोऽभ्यसूयकाः ॥

Given over to self-conceit, hunger
for power, insolence, carnal desire and
anger, these malicious ones hate God
in the bodies of others and in their own.

XVI-18

Not listening to the inner voice and
debasing oneself or doing injury to others is
equivalent to hatred of God, for He abides in
the souls of all men and, indeed, suffers
through them. See also XVII-6, quoted in the
chapter p. 92.

Any code of life based on the satisfaction of mere desire leads to destruction. In deciding what is good and right, let men be guided by the experiences of those who have gone before.

The inheritance of knowledge that good and wise men have left behind as the result of their search for God and Truth is *Shastra*. It is right that each generation of the human race should build on the foundation of the results of the toil of previous generations. Otherwise we must be engaged like Sisyphus rolling the stone up for ever.

य: शास्त्रविधिमुत्सृज्य वर्तते कामकारत: ।
न स सिद्धिमवाप्नोति न सुखं न परां गतिम् ॥

He who disregards the ordinances of the Shastras and follows the promptings of desire is not on the road to the highest goal, nor can he attain spiritual power or worldly happiness.

XVI-23

तस्माच्छास्त्रं प्रमाणं ते कार्याकार्यव्यवस्थितौ ।
ज्ञात्वा शास्त्रविधानोक्तं कर्म कर्तुमिहार्हसि ॥

Therefore, let Shastra be thy guide in determining what ought to be done, or what ought not to be done. Guided by what hath been declared by the ordinances of Shastra, you should engage yourself in work in this world.

XVI-24

CHAPTER X

IDEALS—AUSTERITIES—FOOD

[Adhyaya XVII—Slokas 3, 5-10, 14-16, 20-22.]

EVERY man is born with a particular nature, the result of his *Karma*. According to this is shaped his faith. Yet the faith that we consciously nurse also reacts on us. We should, therefore, set for ourselves good ideals. The action and reaction between natural tendency and chosen ideals are brought out in the following *sloka*. Hope for progress lies in this interaction.

सत्वानुरूपा सर्वस्य श्रद्धा भवति भारत ।
श्रद्धामयोऽयं पुरुषो यो यच्छ्रद्ध: स एव स: ॥

Everyone's faith is fashioned
according to one's essential nature.
Man is made up of his faith; that in
which a man places faith, he too is that.

XVII-3

Not only should we fix our minds on right ideals, but all our activities should be regulated with a view to upward evolution. "Religious" acts, be it sacrifices, austerities, worship or alms-giving, should not be done for ostentation or for attaining selfish ends. There is not only no good but harm in austerities undergone merely for vanity's sake or in the hope of getting some advantage thereby. The mere tormenting of one's flesh is not penance.

अशास्त्रविहितं घोरं तप्यन्ते ये तपो जना: ।
दम्भाहंकारसंयुक्ता: कामरागबलान्विता: ॥

The men who perform severe austerities, unenjoined by the scriptures, out of vanity and self-conceit, impelled by the force of their desires and passions.

XVII-5

कर्षयन्त: शरीरस्थं भूतग्राममचेतस: ।
मां चैवान्त:शरीरस्थं तान्विद्ध्यासुरनिश्चयान् ॥

These foolish men torment the elements forming the bodies, and Me also, dwelling within the body; know these as men of Asuric resolves.

XVII-6

Tapas or austerities may be performed in body, speech or mind. *Tapas* of body consists in conduct marked by rectitude, reverence, continence and compassion. *Tapas* of utterance consists in truthful, gentle and kindly speech, in the study and recital of scriptures. The cultivation of mental equilibrium and purity of thought is *Tapas* of mind. *Tapas* should be practised without desire for any selfish objects and as being good in itself. When done with the object of just gaining the respect of men or for ostentation, it is worthless, and when done in order to hurt others or in a spirit of mere obstinacy, it is wicked.

देवद्विजगुरुप्राज्ञपूजनं शौचमार्जवम् ।
ब्रह्मचर्यमहिंसा च शारीरं तप उच्यते ॥

Worship rendered to the gods, to the twice-born, to the teachers and to the enlightened, clean life, rectitude, continence and non-violence are said to constitute austerity of the body.

XVII-14

अनुद्वेगकरं वाक्यं सत्यं प्रियहितं च यत् ।
स्वाध्यायाभ्यसनं चैव वाङ्मयं तप उच्यते ॥

Speech that causes no annoyance, and which is truthful, loving and beneficial, the study and recitation of the scriptures, these are declared to be austerities of the spoken word.

XVII-15

मनःप्रसादः सौम्यत्वं मौनमात्मविनिग्रहः ।
भावसंशुद्धिरित्येतत्तपो मानसमुच्यते ॥

Tranquillity of mind, gentleness, reticence; self-control, purity of thought, these constitute austerity of the mind.

XVII-16

Giving also is, according to the motive behind it, good, useless or worse. We should give gladly and not grudgingly, and in a spirit of duty and not in expectation of a returning obligation, or even to gain the merit of alms-giving. The *Gita* divides human activities, desires, tastes, and, indeed, everything, into three classes; the first wherein the spirit of truth and harmony dominates is *Sattvik*; the second wherein the urge to action, the passion-nature, dominates is *Rajasik*; the third and, last in the scale is *Tamasik*, wherein inertia dominates.

दातव्यमिति यद्दानं दीयतेऽनुपकारिणे ।
देशे काले च पात्रे च तद्दानं सात्त्विकं स्मृतम् ॥

That gift is classed as pure which is made to one who is not expected to do something in return, and is made with the feeling that the gift is a duty and is also made in the right place and time to a worthy person.

XVII-20

यत्तु प्रत्युपकारार्थं फलमुद्दिश्य वा पुनः ।
दीयते च परिक्लिष्टं तद्दानं राजसं स्मृतम् ॥

That which is given with a view to getting something in return or looking for merit, and what is given grudgingly, are deemed Rajasik gifts.

XVII-21

अदेशकाले यद्दानमपात्रेभ्यश्च दीयते ।
असत्कृतमवज्ञातं तत्तामसमुदाहृतम् ॥

Gifts made without propriety of place and time, and to unworthy persons, disrespectfully or contemptuously, are deemed of the nature of Tamas.

XVII-22

The food we daily take has its effect on our psychology and character. It may be *Sattvik*, good and strengthening to the spirit; or destructive of serenity, passion-producing, *Rajasik;* or wholly bad, causing deterioration of mind and intellect and increasing inertia, *Tamasik*.

आहारस्त्वपि सर्वस्य त्रिविधो भवति प्रिय: ।
यज्ञस्तपस्तथा दानं तेषां भेदमिमं शृणु ॥

The food liked by men is also of three kinds, as also sacrifice, austerity and alms-giving. Hear thou the distinction of these.

XVII-7

आयु:सत्त्वबलारोग्यसुखप्रीतिविवर्धना: ।
रस्या: स्निग्धा: स्थिरा हृद्या आहारा: सात्त्विकप्रिया: ॥

The foods that promote long life and vitality, bodily vigour, health, joy and amiability, which are pleasant to the taste, soft, substantial and satisfying, are liked by Sattvik natures.

XVII-8

कट्वाम्ललवणात्युष्णतीक्ष्णरूक्षविदाहिन: ।
आहारा राजसस्येष्टा दु:खशोकामयप्रदा: ॥

The passionate desire foods that are bitter, sour, saline, over-hot, pungent, dry and burning. These produce sickness, pain and grief.

XVII-9

यातयामं गतरसं पूतिपर्युषितं च यत् ।
उच्छिष्टमपि चामेध्यं भोजनं तामसप्रियम् ॥

Food that is not freshly made,
food that has lost its flavour, stale food,
and food that has gone putrid, leavings
of food and food which is filthy, these
appeal to men of Tamasik nature.

XVII-10

CHAPTER XI

SURRENDER AND GRACE

[Adhyaya IX—Sloka 22. Adhyaya X—Slokas 9-11. Adhyaya XII—Slokas 5-7. Adhyaya XIV—Sloka 26. Adhyaya XVIII—Slokas 62, 64-66.]

THE *Gita* recognizes the difficulty of worship in terms of the Impersonal and Absolute. The aspirant is, therefore, advised to practise contemplation of God in His personal aspect as loving Ruler of the universe. Even keeping Him in mind, let us engage ourselves in all activities, and dedicate all our work to God as service and worship done unto Him. Ultimately it is His Grace alone that can save us, by giving us power of self-control, knowledge and peace, and protecting us from temptation, doubt, weakness and confusion. This aspect of Hindu faith is known as the *Bhakti* path of Salvation. It is, however, not an alternative to, but a complement of, the practice of an unselfish and detached attitude in the performance of the duties that fall to one's lot. There is no question as to which is the more important of the two, the seeking of Grace or the performance of duty. Either may be considered as the primary and the other as the complementary part of the *Gita* teaching.

अनन्याश्चिन्तयन्तो मां ये जनाः पर्युपासते ।
तेषां नित्याभियुक्तानां योगक्षेमं वहाम्यहम् ॥

I take upon Myself the concern for the welfare of those who worship Me with undistracted mind, and have thereby yoked themselves permanently to Divine Spirit.

IX-22

मच्चित्ता मद्गतप्राणा बोधयन्तः परस्परम् ।
कथयन्तश्च मां नित्यं तुष्यन्ति च रमन्ति च ॥

They fill their thoughts with Me, they live for Me, they find their joy and their only satisfaction in constantly conversing and enlightening one another about Me.

X-9

तेषां सततयुक्तानां भजतां प्रीतिपूर्वकम् ।
ददामि बुद्धियोगं तं येन मामुपयान्ति ते ॥

To these, ever-harmonised, loving devotees, I give the *Yoga* of spiritual understanding and thereby they come unto Me.

X-10

तेषामेवानुकम्पार्थमहमज्ञानजं तमः ।
नाशयाम्यात्मभावस्थो ज्ञानदीपेन भास्वता ॥

Out of My compassion for them, dwelling within their souls I dispel the darkness of their ignorance with the shining light of true understanding.

X-11

क्लेशोऽधिकतरस्तेषामव्यक्तासक्तचेतसाम् ।
अव्यक्ता हि गतिर्दुःखं देहवद्भिरवाप्यते ॥

The task of those whose minds
seek to realise the Unmanifest is one
of great difficulty, for the Unmanifest
is hard for the embodied to realise.

XII-5

ये तु सर्वाणि कर्माणि मयि संन्यस्य मत्पराः ।
अनन्येनैव योगेन मां ध्यायन्त उपासते ॥

Those who dedicate all their
actions to Me, and are wholly intent
on attaining Me, and concentrate their
minds in meditation of Me.

XII-6

तेषामहं समुद्धर्ता मृत्युसंसारसागरात् ।
भवामि न चिरात्पार्थ मय्यावेशितचेतसाम् ॥

Those whose minds are fixed
thus on Me, I speedily save them from
being tossed about in the ocean of life
and death.

XII-7

मां च योऽव्यभिचारेण भक्तियोगेन सेवते ।
स गुणान्समतीत्यैतान् ब्रह्मभूयाय कल्पते ॥

He who worships Me with
unswerving devotion crosses the
barriers of inherited qualities and
fashions himself for absorption into the
Eternal.

XIV-26

The following *slokas* are believed to contain the essence of the *Gita* teaching and the last word on the subject. There can be no stronger insistence on complete surrender to God and dependence on His Grace:—

तमेव शरणं गच्छ सर्वभावेन भारत ।
तत्प्रसादात्परां शांतिं स्थानं प्राप्स्यसि शाश्वतम् ॥

Put your trust in Him and have no other thought; by His Grace you will attain supreme peace and the everlasting abode.

XVIII-62

सर्वगुह्यतमं भूयः शृणु मे परमं वचः ।
इष्टोऽसि मे दृढमिति ततो वक्ष्यामि ते हितम् ॥

Listen again to My supreme word, most secret of all. You are dear to me, therefore, I emphatically declare it for your benefit.

XVIII-64

मन्मना भव मद्भक्तो मद्याजी मां नमस्कुरु ।
मामेवैष्यसि सत्यं ते प्रतिजाने प्रियोऽसि मे ॥

Give all your thoughts, your worship, your sacrifice and your salutations to Me, and you shall certainly come to Me; I pledge my troth to you who are dear to Me,

XVIII-65

सर्वधर्मान्परित्यज्य मामेकं शरणं व्रज ।
अहं त्वां सर्वपापेभ्यो मोक्षयिष्यामि मा शुचः ॥

Do not depend on articles of faith
or rules of observance, but surrender
yourself completely to Me; grieve not, I
will liberate you from every sin.

XVIII-66

Nought avails but God and He will save
us without doubt, whatsoever be our sins, if we
grieve for them and surrender ourselves to His
Grace.

CHAPTER XII

THE ONENESS OF EXISTENCE

[Adhyaya V—Slokas 16, 18. Adhyaya VI—Slokas 29-31. Adhyaya VIII—Slokas 9, 10, 12-14, 18-20, 22. Adhyaya XVIII—Slokas 20, 45-49.]

REGULATING conduct, controlling the mind, and dedicating all activities as worship unto the Supreme Being, the aspirant realises in course of time the oneness of all existence. The identification of self with all life and of all with the Divine is the *Jnana,* which the *Gita* wants the disciple to strive to attain, so as to liberate the soul from the enveloping darkness of ignorance. Differences between the cultured and the uncultured, distinctions of high and low and even of one life-form from another, all melt away in the enlarged and clarified vision of the man who attains true enlightenment. Even the "eater of dog's meat" becomes one with the rest.

ज्ञानेन तु तदज्ञानं येषां नाशितमात्मन: ।
तेषामादित्यवज्ज्ञानं प्रकाशयति तत्परम् ॥

When ignorance is dispelled by knowledge of the Self; knowledge shining like the sun reveals the Supreme.

V-16

विद्याविनयसम्पन्ने ब्राह्मणे गवि हस्तिनि ।
शुनि चैव श्वपाके च पण्डिताः समदर्शिनः ॥

Sages look with equal eye on a
Brahmana rich with learning and
culture, or a cow, or an elephant or
even a dog or an eater of dogs.

V-18

सर्वभूतस्थमात्मानं सर्वभूतानि चात्मनि ।
ईक्षते योगयुक्तात्मा सर्वत्र समदर्शनः ॥

The soul, enlightened by Yoga,
sees himself in all beings, and all beings
in himself; all are equal in his eye.

VI-29

यो मां पश्यति सर्वत्र सर्वं च मयि पश्यति ।
तस्याहं न प्रणश्यामि स च मे न प्रणश्यति ॥

He who sees Me in everything,
and sees everything in Me, to him I am
ever present and he is ever present to
Me.

VI-30

सर्वभूतस्थितं यो मां भजत्येकत्वमास्थितः ।
सर्वथा वर्तमानोऽपि स योगी मयि वर्तते ॥

He who has firmly realised unity
and worships Me as abiding in all
beings, howsoever he be engaged, is a
Yogi and abides in Me.

VI-31

सर्वभूतेषु येनैकं भावमव्ययमीक्षते ।
अविभक्तं विभक्तेषु तज्ज्ञानं विद्धि सात्त्विकम् ॥

> When the understanding enables
> one to see an immutable oneness in
> all beings, and an undivided whole in
> all the manifold shapes, know that to
> be the true Light.
>
> XVIII-20

The *Gita* lays down the highest ideals of self-control and realisation of all-embracing oneness. It is not mere philosopher's amusement, but an earnest appeal to men and women to shape their lives according to its teaching and to do so at once. The *Gita* teaching is for the young as well as for the old; for the most busy man of action as for those who have done with the turmoil of life. The *Gita* is a book for all time, no doubt; but even like other holy books, which are for all time, its words must yet be read on the background of the social order of the time and place wherein the book was written. It was not made to be quoted as authority for modern movements. Nor can its inadequacy to serve such a purpose be a just or sensible criticism of it. What the *Gita* lays down is sufficiently emphatic to be helpful as authority even for modern movements of equality. Its insistence in the following *slokas* on the equivalence and nobility of all work should not be misinterpreted as an apology for maintaining the distinctions of high and low based on birth to which they refer, but should be given its just meaning. The caste system and occupations fixed by birth are taken for granted in the book, and teaching is developed thereon. It cannot be interpreted for that reason as a defence of the system for all time. What the *Gita* emphasizes is that everyone should observe the code of honour and perform the duties of his allotted station in society. It lays down that there is in truth no superiority or inferiority in the various duties allotted to various groups in any social order, all being equally necessary of performance for the maintenance of society. It lays down that they should all be performed without neglect or confusion, and in the spirit of unselfish social cooperation; this teaching has equal validity whether the social co-operation demanded be in accordance with the caste system, or any social order that has replaced it or which may be accepted by society in the future. There is no work about which one can say, "this is noble and good, free from all evil, and I shall, therefore, prefer to do it rather than that which has been allotted to me," In every thing to be done in this world, some apparent evil is involved, but there is a purifying and ennobling agent for it all, *viz.*, the unselfish attitude. The teaching that work should be done and done well, not for the gratification of selfish desire but for the carrying on of social life, and that social co-operation is, indeed, worship of God, is applicable to every system of social organisation, be it the most ancient or the most modern. The insistence on co-operation without selfish motives, and the plea that such an attitude of mind ennobles and equalises all tasks should not be misread as a plea for any particular form of social order.

स्वे स्वे कर्मण्यभिरत: संसिद्धिं लभते नर: ।
स्वकर्मनिरत: सिद्धिं यथा विन्दति तच्छृणु ॥

Man reaches proper fulfilment by each being intent on his own duty. Let Me tell you how the goal is attained by him who is intent on his own duty.

XVIII-45

यत: प्रवृत्तिर्भूतानां येन सर्वमिदं ततम् ।
स्वकर्मणा तमभ्यर्च्य सिद्धिं विन्दति मानव: ॥

The performance of one's own duty is worship of Him from Whom have emanated all beings, and by Whom all this is pervaded, and by such worship a man attains the goal.

XVIII-46

श्रेयान् स्वधर्मो विगुण: परधर्मास्त्वनुष्ठितात् ।
स्वभावनियतं कर्म कुर्वन्नाप्नोति किल्बिषम् ॥

Better is one's own duty, though unhonoured, than the work of another even if well performed. He who does the work indicated by his own nature incurs no sin.

XVIII-47

सहजं कर्म कौन्तेय सदोषमपि न त्यजेत् ।
सर्वारम्भा हि दोषेण धूमेनाग्निरिवावृता: ॥

The work to which you are born, though involving defects, ought not to be abandoned. All undertakings, indeed, are clouded by defects as fire by smoke.

XVIII-48

असक्तबुद्धिः सर्वत्र जितात्मा विगतस्पृहः ।
नैष्कर्म्यसिद्धिं परमां संन्यासेनाधिगच्छति ॥

He who holds his inner Spirit
unbound, whatever he may do, whose
self is well-controlled and who is free
from desire, attains by such
renunciation that supreme goal which
is the aim of renunciation of action.

XVIII-49

The aspirant should meditate on the
Absolute and Eternal behind all the
manifestations of birth, life, death and
disappearance. Creation and destruction are
mere appearance and disappearance,
analogous to what a child may see in the
appearance and disappearance of life in the
cycle of day and night. They are but the waking
and sleeping, the day and night of *Brahma*.
When man gets true Light, he realises the
Supreme unity of Existence. The contemplation
and realisation of this supreme oneness is the
end and aim of *Yoga*.

अनन्यचेताः सततं यो मां स्मरति नित्यशः ।
तस्याहं सुलभः पार्थ नित्ययुक्तस्य योगिनः ॥

To him who constantly meditates
upon Me, not letting his thoughts
swerve aside, to him who is ever yoked
to the Spirit, I am easy of attainment.

VIII-14

अव्यक्ताद्व्यक्तयः सर्वाः प्रभवन्त्यहरागमे ।
रात्र्यागमे प्रलीयन्ते तत्रैवाव्यक्तसंज्ञके ॥

From the unmanifested all the manifested issue at the coming of day; at the coming of night they again disappear into what is termed the unmanifested.

VIII-18

भूतग्राम: स एवायं भूत्वा भूत्वा प्रलीयते ।
रात्र्यागमेऽवश: पार्थ प्रभवत्यहरागमे ॥

This totality of life is thus involuntarily brought forth, repeatedly disappearing at the coming of night and appearing at the coming of day.

VIII-19

परस्तस्मात्तु भावोऽन्योऽव्यक्तोऽव्यक्तात्सनातन: ।
य: स सर्वेषु भूतेषु नश्यत्सु न विनश्यति ॥

There exists higher than this unmanifested another unmanifest Entity, ever abiding, which, when all things disappear, is not itself destroyed.

VIII-20

पुरुष: स पर: पार्थ भक्त्या लभ्यस्त्वनन्यया ।
यस्यान्त:स्थानि भूतानि येन सर्वमिदं ततम् ॥

That Transcendent One, in Whom all beings abide, by Whom all this world is pervaded, may be reached by unswerving devotion.

VIII-22

कविं पुराणमनुशासितारमणोरणीयांसमनुस्मरेद्य: ।
सर्वस्य धातारमचिन्त्यरूपमादित्यवर्णं तमस: परस्तात् ॥

He who contemplates on the All-knowing, the Ancient, the Ruler, minuter than the atom, the Supporter of all, of form inconceivable, refulgent as the sun, casting no shadow.

VIII-9

प्रयाणकाले मनसाऽचलेन भक्त्या युक्तो योगबलेन चैव ।
भ्रुवोर्मध्ये प्राणमावेश्य सम्यक् स तं परं पुरुषमुपैति दिव्यम् ॥

At the time of death, with steady mind, full of devotion, by the power of Yoga drawing together his life-energy into the space between the eye-brows, he goes to the Spirit transcendent and divine.

VIII-10

Chapter XIII

ADVAITA AND GITA-DISCIPLINE

A QUESTION may be raised at this stage by those who have only heard of or have a superficial acquaintance with the doctrine of *Advaita*. If the Soul's separate existence is the result of illusion and God alone exists, why should there be this toilsome effort at so-called liberation? Why should we not rest content with knowing the truth that God alone exists? This might well be so, were the illusion a mere optical illusion. The *Maya* has wrought its effect not only on the eyes but on every one of our senses and on our minds, and has produced attachments, passions and turmoils of the soul. Rubbing the eyes alone will not do. We must wake up every atom of our being to the reality, because the illusion goes to the depth of our very being. Again, it is not enough to know that we should wake up. It is necessary actually to wake up. This real and thorough awakening of our being is called liberation, and the process is just the same whether it proceeds on this basis of waking up from an illusion, or is deemed a process of self-purification and liberation of the *soul* as a real and separate entity.

Sense-enjoyments and attachment thereto confirm and add to the illusion. It is necessary to get rid of them in order to dispel the *Maya*. The knowledge gained from the teacher, that God and Soul are one, but for ignorance born of *Maya*, may be an aid in the process of liberation or waking up, but that by itself is not enough. The need for personal effort to free oneself from passions and attachments diminishes as one approaches the goal of true enlightenment, and diminishes in the measure of our progress towards it.

Whether the individual soul be treated as a result of *Maya*, liberation consisting, then, in the removal of the illusion that brought about the idea of individual existence, or whether it be considered that the individual soul is a really separate entity beginningless, free and clothed in matter, which must work out its salvation by fitting itself for being received by God--in either case, the process to be gone through is identical. If the Soul's separate existence is an illusion, attachment to the objects of sense-enjoyment, and lust, greed and anger add to the illusion and must be avoided. With real disillusionment, sins and attachments must automatically cease. Conversely, a pure life and unselfish performance of duties and serenity of mind lead to realisation of the truth behind the veil. Where attachments have not ceased, we may take it that the knowledge is unreal, and that only lip-service is being rendered to theory, and the illusion within is increasing, not diminishing. True *Jnana* can come, and great illusion be dissolved only by the same process as has been prescribed for liberation from *Karma* on the basis of the soul being a separate spiritual entity according to the *Dvaita* Philosophy. Thus it is that the *Gita* is a book of Life for all, irrespective of differing creeds as to the ultimate nature of the individual Soul.

CHAPTER XIV

SEEING GOD

[Adhyaya XI—Slokas 9, 12, 13, 15-18, 38-40, 43, 44.]

THE eleventh chapter of the *Gita* records what may be termed a miracle. Arjuna is enabled to see God as the all-embracing Universal spirit before which the pairs of opposites, of good and evil, pleasure and pain, light and darkness, and the like, disappear. This vision of the Universal was too dazzling for Arjuna to see as a whole, and even what he saw was too awful for sight to bear. Literally Arjuna was given the divine eye to enable him to see the trans-dichotomous *Visvarupa*, which transcends the Relative and the Partial. The meaning of this is that the aspiring soul may catch a glimpse of God, the Universal Immanent Being, when by a pure and dedicated life, and by the practice of serenity and constant meditation, the *Yogi* succeeds in merging his self in the Universe and realises the ultimate oneness of all existence.

Sanjaya, who narrated the events of the battle to the blind Emperor Dhritarashtra, describes the vision that was unfolded to

Arjuna. It was of God, the All, that embraces the whole universe not excluding either of the pairs of opposites, good and evil, beautiful and ugly, sweet and terrible, pleasant and painful.

संजय उवाच

एवमुक्त्वा ततो राजन् महायोगेश्वरो हरि: ।
दर्शयामास पार्थाय परमं रूपमैश्वरम् ॥

Sanjaya said:

Having said this, O King, the great Lord of Yoga, Hari, showed to Partha His transcendent Form as Lord of the Universe.

XI-9

दिवि सूर्यसहस्रस्य भवेद्युगपदुत्थिता ।
यदि भा: सदृशी सा स्याद् भासस्तस्य महात्मन: ॥

If a thousand suns could blaze out together in the sky, that might perhaps be something like the glory of that great manifestation.

XI-12

तत्रैकस्थं जगत्कृत्स्नं प्रविभक्तमनेकधा ।
अपश्यद्देवदेवस्य शरीरे पाण्डवस्तदा ॥

Then the Pandava beheld the whole of the multitudinous universe, brought together and manifested as one single form in the body that the God of all Gods then assumed.

XI-13

When this great vision was unfolded, Arjuna burst into a hymn of praise.

पश्यामि देवांस्तव देव देहे सर्वांस्तथा भूतविशेषसंघान् ।
ब्रह्माणमीशं कमलासनस्थमृषींश्च सर्वानुरगांश्च दिव्यान् ॥

In Thy form, O God, all the gods
I see, and crowds of all grades of beings;
Brahma, the Lord, upon His lotus-seat,
all the Rishis, and the serpent-gods.

XI-15

अनेकबाहूदरवक्त्रनेत्रं पश्यामि त्वां सर्वतोऽनन्तरूपम् ।
नान्तं न मध्यं न पुनस्तवादिं पश्यामि विश्वेश्वर विश्वरूप ॥

I see Thee everywhere, with
arms, trunks, mouths and eyes,
multitudinous, of shape limitless. I see
no beginning, middle, nor end of Thee,
Lord of the Universe, Form All-
embracing.

XI-16

किरीटिनं गदिनं चक्रिणं च तेजोराशिं सर्वतो दीप्तिमन्तम् ।
पश्यामि त्वां दुर्निरीक्ष्यं समन्तात् दीप्तानलार्कद्युतिमप्रमेयम् ॥

Immeasurable, dazzling, mass of
splendour, like the sun or the blazing
fire, with lustre issuing in all directions,
and with crown, mace and discus, I see
Thee.

XI-17

त्वमक्षरं परमं वेदितव्यं त्वमस्य विश्वस्य परं निधानम् ।
त्वमव्ययः शाश्वतधर्मगोप्ता सनातनस्त्वं पुरुषो मतो मे ॥

Thou art the ever-abiding, the
Transcendent, the Goal of all
knowledge. Thou art the supreme

abode of this universe; Thou art the changeless Guardian of Eternal Nature.

XI-18

त्वमादिदेव: पुरुष: पुराणस्त्वमस्य विश्वस्य परं निधानम् ।
वेत्ताऽसि वेद्यं च परं च धाम त्वया ततं विश्वमनन्तरूप ॥

First of the Gods, Primeval Spirit, Supreme abode of all that lives; Thou art the Knower and Thou art that which is to be known, Thou art Heaven transcendent, Thou art spread over the universe, O Thou of shape unending!

XI-38

वायुर्यमोऽग्निर्वरुण: शशांक: प्रजापतिस्त्वं प्रपितामहश्च: ।
नमो नमस्तेऽस्तु सहस्रकृत्व: पुनश्च भूयोऽपि नमो नमस्ते ॥

Thou art Vayu, Yama, Agni, Varuna and the Moon. Thou art the progenitor of the universe, the Grandsire. Prostrations to Thee! A thousand prostrations! Again and again, I bow to Thee.

XI 39

नम: पुरस्तादथ पृष्ठतस्ते नमोऽस्तु ते सर्वत एव सर्व ।
अनन्तवीर्यामितविक्रमस्त्वं सर्वं समाप्नोषि ततोऽसि सर्व: ॥

I bow in front of Thee, I bow to Thee behind. Prostrations on every side to Thee, O All. Of energy boundless, measureless in strength, Thou art the completion of everything; Thou art everything Thyself.

XI-40

पिताऽसि लोकस्य चराचरस्य त्वमस्य पूज्यश्च गुरुर्गरीयान् ।
न त्वत्समोऽस्त्यभ्यधिक: कुतोऽन्यो लोकत्रयेऽप्यप्रतिमप्रभाव ॥

Thou art the world's Father, of all that moves, and of all that stands, adorable, the greatest Guru. There is none like Thee. Who can surpass Thee, unequalled in power in all the three worlds?

XI-43

तस्मात्प्रणम्य प्रणिधाय कायं प्रसादये त्वामहमीशमीड्यम् ।
पितेव पुत्रस्य सखेव सख्यु: प्रिय: प्रियायार्हसि देव सोढुम् ॥

Therefore, I fall prostrate and offer salutations to Thee; worthy Lord, I seek Thy grace; Thou shouldst bear with me as father does with son, as friend with friend, as lover with his beloved.

XI-44

CHAPTER XV

CONCLUSION

WE may now summarise our studies.

We are born with certain qualities and potentialities of body and mind as a result of the previous activities and attachments of the soul. This holds us in a strong grip. But we have the freedom to liberate ourselves. But soul's activities in its present body decide its future, whether it be partial or complete liberation from past *Karma* or further bondage. The Grace of God can bring about liberation, however great may be the previous bondage. This is so, not only because of the inherent power of Grace, but also because the soul's efforts to obtain that Grace have themselves, like other motions of the mind, *Karmic* potency. The *Gita* teaches what these efforts should be, to which it gives the name of *Yoga*.

The *Yoga* of the *Gita* is a progressive and multiple process. There is no loss in attempt and failure, as every sincere effort is a gain in itself. It consists of:

(1) Control of the senses and purity of conduct, and regulation of the routine of life, worship, work, food, sleep, etc.;

(2)   Unselfish, but nonetheless attentive,
      performance of the duties to which one is
      called by one's natural fitness and by
      reason of one's place in the social
      organisation;

(3)   Cultivation of true detachment and an
      even spirit in the face of success or
      difficulty or failure, or causes for joy, grief
      or disappointment;

(4)   Vigilant control of the motions of the
      mind, and the elimination of passions
      that disturb it—lust, anger and greed;

(5)   Periodical turning of the mind inwards,
      for silent, concentrated meditation; and

(6)   Surrender to God's grace.

Each of these aspects of Yoga may be
emphasised and given a separate name, such
as *Sankhya Yoga, Karma Yoga, Jnana Yoga,
Sannyasa Yoga, Adhyatma Yoga*, or *Bhakti
Yoga*. But, in practice, they are all mutually
connected and inseparable; and so, all are
combined in the *Gita* and brought together in
one organic synthesis.

It is possible that the reader of these
pages may say: The ideal of the *Gita* is good,
but it is impracticable; ordinary men can never
hope to attain it. What good is it then to men in
this world of reality?

This question may be asked not only in
respect of the *Gita* teaching, but of every great
religion of the world. All the faiths and all the
scriptures present ideals that are impossible of

complete attainment in the work-a-day world. For example, who can maintain that the life and teachings of Christ can be truly and fully followed by the Christians that revere and worship Him as God? The same is the case of the Koranic or the Buddhistic teachings. Yet it is true that every one of these religions has not only stirred great men's hearts and given strength to their souls, but is the daily bread of life to millions of common mortals, who otherwise would have been like beasts of the field.

The *Bible*, the *Koran* and the *Gita* are like lamps that light our paths in darkness. We cast our own shadows on our path in spite of the lantern in our hands; so, every besetting temptation, doubt, fear or difficulty throws its dark shadow, in spite of the light we carry; and the way is a chequered pattern of light and shadow. Still, holding the light firmly in our hands we may walk fairly safely. If we let the light go out, we should be lost in the jungle. Not every one that swears by a book may be able to follow everything that is said therein; but if every one tries, society grows round the ideals. When a whole people revere certain ideals, life is furnished with standards of conduct that save men from becoming mere beasts of the field and they are held together. That we cannot be perfect is no objection to hold the light firmly in our hands, so that we may see our way amidst the shadows. Helped by Religion, men live like men even though, too often, erring. Why, are not the rules of mere physical hygiene impossible of being followed to perfection? No one thinks of discarding the rules of physical hygiene as a string of impossibilities and counsels of perfection; but wise men and women try as far as they can to abide by them, and we profit thereby. So should it be also with the care and protection of the Soul.

नेहाभिक्रमनाशोऽस्ति प्रत्यवायो न विद्यते ।

स्वल्पमप्यस्य धर्मस्य त्रायते महतो भयात् ॥

There is nothing like waste of effort in this, nor is there any danger of retrogression by reason of short-comings in practice. Even a little of this Dharma saves men from the great evil.

II-40

INDEX OF SLOKAS QUOTED